BLUE GRIT

A LIFE ON THE HUMANITARIAN FRONTLINES
OF THE
UNITED NATIONS

ULF T. KRISTOFFERSSON

Blue Grit: A Life on the Humanitarian Frontlines of the United Nations
Copyright ©2015 by Ulf T. Kristoffersson
Photographs from the author's collection
All rights reserved.
www.bluegrit.net

Publisher's Cataloging-in-Publication Data
provided by Five Rainbows Services

Kristoffersson, Ulf T.
  Blue grit : a life on the humanitarian frontlines of the United Nations / Ulf T. Kristoffersson.
     pages cm
     Includes index.
     ISBN: 978-1-5052-9834-5 (pbk.)
     1. United Nations—Officials and employees—Biography. 2. Humanitarian assistance. 3. Public health. 4. Disaster relief. 5. United Nations—Peacekeeping forces. I. Title.
JZ4973.5 .K57 2014
341.23—dc23

Designed by Gia Giasullo
Printed by CreateSpace

*To Christina and Linnéa
& to Karl-Robert, Alexandra and Alexander
& to all the grandchildren and great-grandchildren
who have not yet heard my stories.*

BLUE GRIT

A LIFE ON THE
HUMANITARIAN FRONTLINES
OF THE
UNITED NATIONS

PROLOGUE 1

PART 1
EYES IN THE JUNGLE

Full Circle: Aranyaprathet 9
Not Ouagadougou 13
On the Brink of an Abyss 17
The Year Before Year Zero 21
Putting Phnom Penh Behind Me 31
The Border Operation 37
The Land Bridge 53

PART 2
THE MAKING OF A FIELD OFFICER

True Grit 63
A Swedish Viking in Rio 65
Training for War and Peace 73
Artemis Road 79
First Taste of Africa 87

PART 3
CHILD SURVIVAL

Ethiopia 111
Sahel 121
Lifeline Sudan 131

PART 4
FROM SHIELD TO TARGET

Refugee Roots 143
Somalia Spills Over 147
The Pain of Mogadishu 155
Rwanda, Failure to Protect 161
Uganda, Aftermath of Genocide 165
Burundi, Point Blank 171

PART 5
PROVIDING FOR PEACEKEEPING

Bhopinder Singh 181
An International Security Risk 183
Resolution 1308 187

EPILOGUE 197

ACKNOWLEDGMENTS 201

PROLOGUE

EVERY YEAR ON OCTOBER 24, the world celebrates an international holiday. It was on this day in 1945 that the allied victors of the Second World War ratified a document they called a "World Security Charter." Prepared in five languages and signed by more than two-hundred representatives of fifty countries, the charter was a collective response to a half-century that had seen two global conflagrations. It called for the formation of a new set of international institutions in which every nation-state might participate in a forum of mutual respect and political engagement – a so-called United Nations in which cooperation would trump confrontation on the world stage. The founding charter's lofty commitments included the intent to "save succeeding generations from the scourge of war … {and} to promote social progress and better standards of life."

Half a world away, I was celebrating my own birthday with far less fanfare and much more modest ambitions. But in the decades since the United Nations and I both arrived on earth, our histories have melded. I have granted the UN almost forty years of my professional life; to its fundamental ideals, I continue to give my lifelong commitment.

The UN Charter has not been altered in seventy years. There have been no amendments, revisions, retractions or repeals. It remains, on paper, as hopeful and unachievable as on that halcyon day in 1945 when the world declared peace and put pen to what the former US President Herbert Hoover termed a "Magna Carta of peace and security."

But the UN itself has changed greatly over the latter 20th century and first decades of the new millennium. And how could it not? The United Nations, after all, is a community—a human community committed to humanity. The UN changes along with the men and women who serve it, both at headquarters and in far-flung postings. The UN is in flux, as are the nation-states that make up its members. It is a living, breathing organism, changing all the time. As the peace of 1945 gave way to the tensions of the Cold War and the challenges of post-colonial liberation movements, the UN's mandated neutrality depended more and more on the commitment of its cadres. That is to say – a high-minded institution had to hold its own against men and women of many different minds. As Jeremy Greenstock, a former UN Representative from Great Britain put it: The United Nations represents "the whole range of human failings played out at the global level."

I, too, have changed in the years since the historic founding. This is the story of how the United Nations shaped my life. It is an interpretation of a remarkable institution based on a personal experience of that institution's growing pains. I cannot claim as many life lessons as the United Nations itself, which is tasked with every global challenge imaginable. But I owe my entire worldview to lessons learned serving the organization; the first being that nothing is learned without mistakes.

I believe that I have made a contribution to the world in this capacity, however modest. Certainly I have contributed mistakes. I am just one of many committed international civil servants whose actions tell the real story of the United Nations. That story is sometimes heroic and sometimes terribly disappointing. I recognize the impact of politics both petty and grand, of the internal squabbles, and of our own human failings on the UN's collective work. I celebrate them all – for as I have argued, the United Nations is a human community – for better or worse.

I am a veteran of the United Nations system, but I do not claim to be an expert. I have never sat down and learned the history of the institution; rather, I took part in the very events that shaped its history. Idealistic rhetoric aside, the United Nations is not a single entity, but a complex system – a network of agencies, programmes, and funds that share common goals: to mitigate the effects of natural and manmade emergencies and to advance the health of men, women and children worldwide; to promote education, social inclusion, and human rights; and to prevent war through peacebuilding and peacekeeping. The people who do that work can be organized in working groups and flow charts; or they can be given tribute through narratives like this one. The UN I hope to introduce to my readers is not the UN of endless acronyms, inter-agency bureaucracies, and endless red tape, but the UN of vaccinators, refuge providers, educators, builders and advocates.

As a visiting professor at both American and European universities, I frequently encounter misgivings and misconceptions among young students interested in international development about the United Nations. Some of these concerns I share: Yes, the safety of millions is often highjacked by political forces in the Security Council. Yes, the largesse of nations has sometimes been misappropriated by bureaucracy, bloat and corruption. But to focus on the flaws in the system is to overlook the strength: Rancor and disagreement in the Security Council is expressed in words, not bullets. Funding diverted in-country is still funding that has been designated specifically for the purpose of advancing humanitarian principals. Without the UN we would not have a Universal Declaration of Rights to defend, a Convention on the Rights of the Child to standardize, nor a General Assembly to serve as a forum in which any nation – no matter how small or how powerful – has a voice.

I have written this book drawing on the events and people that have stayed sharpest in my mind over many decades. Those who have faded somewhat have received new names and (forgive me) may find themselves placed in dates slightly obscured by my own chronology. I blame not the fog of war, but the fog of too many wars, too many crises, and too many repetitions of the same unfolding humanitarian dilemmas. I have recorded the events to the best of my ability, consulting many a contradictory history to refresh my mind of dates and places along the way.

Ultimately, I hope only to convey a representative survey of "the good, the bad and the ugly" of the United Nations. In truth, there has been a great deal of *good*, a predictable measure of *bad*, and some appalling instances of *ugly*. But even in moments when the UN has appeared most blemished by failure, most disfigured by crimes it did not commit, there is also a spot of beauty. For any effort - no matter how quixotic - to find a universal discourse, maintain global peace and advance the well being of humanity cannot hide its real beauty for long.

THAILAND

- Vientiane
- Bangkok
- Aranyaprathet

Gulf of Thailand

LAOS

PART 1

EYES IN THE JUNGLE

CAMBODIA

Phnom Penh

VIETNAM

Saigon

South China Sea

CHAPTER 1

Full Circle: Aranyaprathet

I HAD BEEN HERE BEFORE. Aranyaprathet - a quiet border post that, like so many demarcations around the world, presented little physical indication of the vast difference between life on one side and life on the other. But in the late 1970's, at this particular border, that difference was stark.

I was standing in Thailand, a country that had spent the past decade as a transit zone, launching pad, observation post and R&R destination. As the United States' closest ally in Indochina, Thailand was a known entity. No matter that it was the hub of uncountable covert operations, it was a place that held little mystery for me. In contrast was the landscape before me: Cambodia, shrouded in silence since April 1975, when the unrelenting army of the Khmer Rouge sent the last foreigners scurrying across the border and then closed the country in a hermetically sealed hell.

Four and a half years earlier, I had stood on this same border waiting for two colleagues, shaken and grateful for their safety, to emerge from the jungle with the message that our work in Cambodia was over. And now I was back, in Aranyaprathet.

I had arrived the day before and spent the night in a dank, humid hotel that, having seen no clientele for years, had moldered into windowless disrepair. Well before dawn, I was summoned by the local commander of the Thai army and escorted to the border, which was as quiet as it had been on that day in 1975. But something was breathing in the jungle beyond, and this rank and file military man and I were its only witnesses.

Ten months had passed since the invading Vietnamese had dislodged the Khmer Rouge regime, but the Thai authorities were only now getting confirmation of the event the world had been anticipating: the survivors of the Khmer Rouge killing fields were on the move. Hundreds of thousands of people were headed for the only certain exit out of the tortured country, the western border; and the Thai government needed assistance in welcoming them.

That may not have been exactly how my monosyllabic partner put it as we watched the sun rise on the hazy distance of jungle, but the understatement was implicit. We were on the brink of a humanitarian emergency of historic proportions, but we spoke of it in euphemisms. Then we fell silent and watched as the jungle revealed its apparition. It took me a moment to understand what I was seeing – not an optical illusion or the reflection of sunrise against the dark foliage, but the steady gaze of eyes in the jungle. I held my breath as they multiplied, emerged and revealed themselves as living beings with lifeless expressions. Men, women and children, too frail and gaunt to speak, staggered out from under the canopy and made their painful way towards us. Many fell before they could cross the last yards to freedom. Many did not rise again.

Ten thousand refugees arrived at the border at Aranyaprathet that day and went no further. They were in urgent need of medical attention, food and water. We called for immediate resources and personnel – the Thai soldier on his radio and I on the only operating telephone in kilometers. Within a week the International Committee of the Red Cross (ICRC) and its larger localized network, the International Federation of Red Cross and Red Crescent Societies, had joined us at the border, which was now a makeshift refugee camp with several hundred thousand inhabitants and more than a hundred aid workers.

But we had only just begun. The 750-kilometer stretch along the Thai-Cambodia border would eventually become home to 700,000 Cambodian nationals, or Khmers, as they are known ethnically. The weeklong scouting mission to the border for which I had been dipatched would turn into a two and a half year mission.

The Cambodian refugee crisis of 1979 was among the greatest challenges the international humanitarian community had tackled since World War II. It was, initially, overwhelming in size. Later, it became a morass of conflicting agendas and a textbook case in the difficulties of isolating humanitarian aid from geopolitics. It was my first evidence that the strength of the United Nations as the world's largest humanitarian organization comes more from its humanity than from its organization.

CHAPTER 2
Not Ouagadougou

INDOCHINA WAS THE LAST PLACE I wanted to go when I signed up to join the United Nations in 1974. I was a dauntless twenty-nine-year-old. I was well travelled, combat-trained and geopolitically informed. I knew I wanted to see the world and to serve the UN— an institution to which I felt a personal connection since I was born on the eve of its own birthday. I also knew that being posted to Southeast Asia while the Vietnam War ran out its ignominious clock was a surefire way to blunt my enthusiasm for the future I envisioned. So when I interviewed to become a Junior Programme Officer at the United Nations Children's Emergency Fund (UNICEF), I steered my thoughts and answers far from that corner of the globe.

There was no shortage of possible posts at that time. UNICEF, founded in 1946 to provide for destitute children in post-war Europe, had grown rapidly over the quarter century. By 1970 it had a presence in more than fifty countries. The mission, too, had expanded. UNICEF was still at its best in emergencies, but as the UN agency tasked with improving the health and welfare of mothers and children alike, the organization had adopted a wider mandate, a diversified range of interventions and, necessarily, a growing staff in the field. More than just a provider of foreign aid, UNICEF was becoming a catalyst of global development and a strong advocate for children's rights.

Of all the UN branches, I was attracted to UNICEF because of its reputation as an organization of absolute neutrality, free of the political hijackings that plagued the United Nations in its signature role as peacekeeper and arbiter. UNICEF did not require a vote in the Security Council or a resolution from the General Assembly to bring its expertise to any country that wanted to enhance education, nutrition or health services for its people. It only required an invitation. Indeed, Henry Labouisse, UNICEF's executive director from 1965 until 1979, made it a directive that the agency would not predicate aid on social conditions or good governance. UNICEF representatives during the Cold War presented their credentials to socialist governments, democratic parliaments, presidents in thrall to Moscow, puppets propped up by Washington, and opportunistic dictators who changed their patrons every week. I was among those ambassadors, sometimes shaking bloodstained hands to ensure that my own were not tied when it came time to deliver lifesaving aid to victims of tyranny. Labouisse's insistence that child welfare come before ideology is what allowed UNICEF to gain the support of 120 governments worldwide and the commendation of the Nobel Committee that "compassion knows no national boundaries," when it awarded the organization the Nobel Peace Prize in 1965.

It wasn't out of some pacifist or ideological dogma that I rejected Southeast Asia when it came time for my posting. It was, quite simply, self-interest. The Vietnam War, it seemed, had taken the whole world captive, and I had no desire to be a literal casualty as well as an indirect one. Washington's "domino theory" had condemned the whole region to an uncertain future. The North Vietnamese offensive that would end the war was still a year away when it came time for me to start my UNICEF posting, but the conflict had taken on a larger life through proxy wars in Laos and Cambodia that pit China and the Soviet Union, superpowers with relations as problematic as any in the Cold War, against each other. In short, it was a complicated and terribly bloody arena. Here was a conflict between not two, but three superpowers, and peace was nowhere in sight.

I knew instinctively that it was a fraught environment for humanitarian work, and at the time, I wanted to stay as far away as possible.

Let it be East Africa, I whispered to myself - a region I had explored and loved as a younger man. *Let it be Latin America,* I encouraged my interviewers, impressing upon them my mastery of English as though that would be helpful anywhere south of Miami. In the end, they said I would be posted to Upper Volta. I closed my eyes and summoned up the map of the African Sahel, resting my imagination on the landlocked country today called Burkina Faso, but known until 1984 by its French colonial name. I mentally shuffled through the deck of flashcards that my Grandmother would play with me as a child: *Upper Volta, bordered to the north by Mali. Home to the Mande and the Mossi. Farmers in a drought-prone region.* I imagined a slow-moving African republic where all was quiet in 1974, halfway through its second decade of independence. Quiet, that is, except for the occasional squabble over a constitution in progress. But even that civil disturbance would only be felt in the capital – Ouagadougou. I let the name roll around in my mouth, delighting in its exotic secrets. *Ouagadougou.*

"Sign me up," I said.

And so I began packing for Upper Volta in West Africa. When I got a call one week later from UNICEF headquarters informing me that my duty station had been changed, as there was a much more urgent need for human resources in Phnom Penh than in Upper Volta, I was momentarily speechless. "Phnom Penh" did not have the same ring as "Ouagadougou." And, from what I gathered in the news, Cambodia was the hottest spot in the Mekong Delta. Long considered a "sideshow" in the broader Indochina conflict, Cambodia in 1974 was fully out of the shadows and bouncing around in the ring.

But I understood that the United Nations was not an organization for those only half-committed. I looked down at the gear I had readied for my Sahel posting and asked the personnel man on the other end of the phone: "How's the weather in Phnom Penh?"

CHAPTER 3

On the Brink of an Abyss

WHEN I LEFT FOR MY FIRST CIVILIAN POSTING as a United Nations servant, it was not my first venture beyond home. In my short life I had already experienced gunfire on a disputed Mediterranean island, the tempest of an Atlantic storm on open water, the majesty of giraffes on the Serengeti plain, and the commanding views from the summit of Kilimanjaro. I was sixteen when I first reeled from the kaleidoscope of colours that was Rio de Janeiro during Carnival; I was still in university when I breathed the heady bouquet of the markets of Dar es Salaam. So when I boarded a flight for Thailand *en route* to Cambodia in the spring of 1974, I reckoned myself well schooled in urban chaos and the physical press of densely populated places.

But nothing prepared me for Bangkok. This was my first time in Asia, the continent that I would call home for the next eight years, and it was just as foreign to me as the furthest planet. The sensory impact alone of the place was incredible.

Young as I was, I was susceptible to the enthusiasm and false pride that the novelty of travel sometimes indulges. The notion that I had somehow "discovered" this exotic place was hard to shake, but the locals were helpful in keeping my self-grandeur in check. Especially the girls who haunted the bars at night, assuring me: "Hey handsome, you number one," along with an offer to let me buy them a whiskey. If I demurred, they would shrug and cut me back down to size: "You number ten."

I stayed in Bangkok for three days, just long enough to distract myself from the nagging truth that I had arrived in the eye of a militant storm. I allowed myself to relax and enjoy my new colleagues, field officers who knew their way around the hedonistic pleasures of Bangkok as well as any American GI on leave. Those in the know told me what to expect from Phnom Penh, the capital of a country that was on the brink of an abyss. Communist rebels, the Khmer Rouge, had occupied 85 percent of the country, I learned. The government's National Defense forces were penned up in Phnom Penh, and no amount of American arms would propel them out to retake the country. It was just a matter of time before the takeover was complete and Cambodia fell, the next domino, into the communist sphere of influence.

On a muggy April morning, I joined an eclectic mix of passengers at Bangkok's Don Mueang airport headed for Phnom Penh, a city starved for staples but glutted with visitors like my fellow travelers: spies, war correspondents, hookers and opportunists. We boarded the aircraft with trepidation. It was an ancient Royal Air Cambodge Caravelle, a relic from Air France that appeared to have forgone maintenance since the French quit their colony twenty years earlier. I took my seat and, after a rather alarming takeoff, I found myself engrossed in the unfolding landscape below, a quilt of rice paddies and jungle. In less than an hour, Pochentong Airport came into view. It was a harrowing sight – a short tarmac lined with aircraft more pathetic than our own Caravelle. The dozen charred skeletons of planes that had been shot down by the Khmer Rouge rebels or abandoned by ground crews lacking equipment to put out the fires of crash landings should have been my first clue as to just how dysfunctional a duty station I was joining.

But I had little time to reflect because our own plane was under fire. The pilots, whose skill I give thanks for to this day, climbed steeply out of range of the rebel firearms and circled, waiting for a lull in the shooting. When it came, we plunged into a desperate dive, our descent accompanied by screams and a few more wretched reactions. Our wild landing was followed by a highly expedited debarkation as we ran like rabbits for the safety of the ramshackle terminal. Inside, I was met by a young man wearing a flak jacket and crash helmet. He was Paul Ignatieff, a Canadian, the grandson of a Russian count, and the UNICEF representative in Cambodia. He was not much older than I, and he had arrived in the city just a few months earlier.

"Welcome to Phnom Penh," he said, handing me a flak jacket and helmet, my UNICEF-issued uniform for the mean streets of the capital.

The name *Ouagadougou* had vanished in the muggy heat.

CHAPTER 4

The Year Before Year Zero

As my new boss and I were driven valiantly, if somewhat recklessly, through the city, I tried to reconcile the information he was giving me with the story I was seeing out the window.

UNICEF Cambodia, Ignatieff explained, had been operating since 1964, when Crown Prince Sihanouk kicked the US aid agency, USAID, out of the country in retaliation for America's refusal to guarantee Cambodia's neutrality in the deepening international war in Vietnam. Invited to fill the gap left by the American *persona non grata* development experts, UNICEF had been running successful education programmes in Cambodia until internal conflict upended the country. A coup in 1970 led by General Lon Nol was the beginning of a tragic end for Cambodia. Outraged by his General's duplicity, the deposed Prince chose to back a small band of leftist extremists to retake power. They dressed in black but called themselves the "Red Khmers" – the Khmer Rouge.

"You can see where that has led us," said Ignatieff, nodding at the makeshift camps lining the road in the city center. After years of fighting, the Khmer Rouge had successfully occupied all of the countryside, herding hundreds of thousands of rural Khmer into the last bastion of Lon Nol's forces – the capital. Phnom Penh, a city of 175,000 before the war, had swelled to an urban refugee camp of nearly two million. The displaced

Cambodians had left behind the fertile fields that were the country's food supply and were now sheltering in temples, schools and public squares. Having fled the violence of war, these miserable people still lived with its destructive force on a daily basis. Bombs rained on the city, hunger stalked its streets, and the black-garbed army of fanatical rebels was visible directly across the Mekong River.

What on earth are we supposed to be doing here? I wondered as we weaved through the city's chaos. In the months to come I would ask the question aloud many times a day, as would my colleagues. We never had a better answer than *waiting for things to get better*. Because it seemed things could not possibly get worse.

In point of fact, what I was doing was perhaps the most understandable task in the UNICEF office. Aside from Ignatieff, who as the Representative was the in-country boss, there were four other international staffers. Kul Gautam, a diminutive soft-spoken Nepali academic, had been there the longest, having arrived in September 1973. In later years, Gautam would serve UNICEF as the Deputy Executive Director. But in those last months before the fall of Phnom Penh, Gautam was, like me, just keeping his head above water in his first duty post. The office was also staffed by Joseph Acar, a Lebanese national who ran our finances such as they were, and by Wendy Bjork of Great Britain. Ignatieff had also hired a dozen Cambodians to facilitate operations, and now he was tasking me, a greenhorn and a junior assistant programme officer, to manage the emergency supply depots.

Of course this late in the game, with the city in a near chokehold and thousands of homeless, hungry, sick women and children arriving daily with just the clothes on their backs, the emergency supply chain was the only UNICEF operation of relevance. The United Nations' presence had been declining steadily as the rebels closed in on the Phnom Penh. The long-term work of agencies like the United Nations Development Programme (UNDP) and the Food and Agriculture Organization (FAO) had come to a standstill. Only basic humanitarian relief was applicable. And I, the lowest man on the totem pole, was at the head of a critical lifeline.

When I arrived, our supplies were still being delivered from Vietnam up the Mekong River by a motley fleet of barges including one captained by a brash Swede by the name of Krister, who had run supplies in hot spots the world over. The general assumption was that in addition to the huge profits my fellow countr man was pulling in for his high-risk venture, there was CIA funding behind his operation. Having surrendered Vietnam, Washington was now funneling arms and resources to Lon Nol, not so much to rebuff the horrors of the Khmer Rouge, which were as yet unknown, but as a counterweight to Hanoi, which was backing the Cambodian rebels.

My job as the operations officer was to meet the boats and to oversee the transport of the relief items – baby formula, medicine, mosquito nets and blankets – to distribution points in the city or to the UNICEF warehouse on the outskirts oftown. One morning, I arrived at the port to find the river empty. I waited for hours before the Swedish captain's tug (by then the last craft to brave the treacherous journey) appeared downriver. The boat's wheelhouse, I saw, was gone. It had been completely shot off by rebel mortars. The captain described this near brush, and then he let me know that this would be UNICEF's last delivery down the Mekong.

"That's it for me," he shrugged. Not even a complete monopoly on Phnom Penh river trade could entice him to stay on the Mekong with its banks bristling with firearms.

I never heard what became of the hotshot Captain Krister, but from that day on, my routine was to rise early and to make the forty-minute drive to the airport in the hope that a supply flight had managed to land safely. From day to day I never knew who would be controlling the access road to the airport –the Khmer Rouge or the government forces, so I always drove in my flak jacket and helmet. On arrival, I would quickly load up the vehicle and get the hell out – if indeed a supply flight had landed. More than once I observed, instead, an empty runway strewn with valuable artifacts – the possessions of an elite whose flight had been arrested mid-air. The only operational supply depots left in the capital were those of UNICEF and the Red Cross. We had become the only source of bandages, medical supplies, saline and baby formula, and our target population was no longer just the city … but the whole country.

Though my days were filled with ferrying supplies, there were demands even more urgent that fell to those of us who had working vehicles in a city under bombardment. I quickly became part of an *ad hoc* ambulance crew. Though the foreign-funded NGOs had pulled most of their staff some months earlier, there were still a handful of stalwart aid workers who, under the auspices of CARE, World Vision, and the Red Cross, were doing whatever they could to lessen the misery. I joined them on regular rounds to ferry the sick, the wounded and the dead to the few functioning hospitals and clinics in the city.

One of these hospitals was located near the UNICEF supply depot. The Khmer-Soviet Friendship Hospital was a heroic facility that had little to show for its former friendship with the Soviets. It kept its doors open despite constant collateral damage. Designed to accommodate about 500 patients, the facility was serving thousands, almost all of them casualties of war, not disease. There was simply no room for sickness in the wards and open-air surgeries where on more than one occasion, I witnessed soldiers demanding expedited service from the staff with a gun to the head. It was never easy entering its courtyard: a wailing scene of wounded, suffering, desperate people. The humidity and heat played hell on triage. Infections bred maggots that I winced to witness, even after a doctor assured me that the repulsive things actually helped the patient heal by eating away the rotten flesh. The ability to remain positive in the face of such an inferno of misery and hopelessness was a shared strength of those doctors and nurses, who both amazed and inspired me. The Soviet Friendship Hospital in Phnom Penh came as close to Dante's Inferno as any place I had encountered on earth. The miracle is that some of its patients emerged from its gaping black stench alive.

As international civil servants, my colleagues and I were better housed and fed than most of the people we were there to serve. Though we all held passports in our pockets that suggested (but did not actually guarantee) we could leave at will, the foreign community was just as physically and emotionally drained from the chaos of the city as the Cambodians we lived among.

My home - invisible from street level, so covered as it was in sandbags - sheltered nearly a dozen people, friends and neighbors of my cook. I slept under the staircase to make room for these people who had no home in their own homeland. My sleeping nook also provided some protection from the constant artillery raining down on the compound of the Defense Forces' headquarters, where my house was rather unluckily located. We relied on generators, as the rebels had long since cut the electricity grid. Fuel for the generators, of course, was also a scarce commodity.

As the intensity of the rocket attacks on Phnom Penh increased, our colleagues in Bangkok and Geneva and New York were actively preparing for the new rebel government. There were contingency plans at all levels of the organization – strategies for a quick implementation of post-conflict relief, reconstruction and resettlement when the Khmer Rouge seized power. For our part, we saw our duty as providing what we could to the displaced refugees, protecting our colleagues, and following the directives of headquarters.

In this waiting game that became more urgent in the first months of 1975, I watched more United Nations colleagues head for the exits, and I cleaved more and more to my madcap journalist friends and the distraction of seeking respite from hardship. When a new restaurant opened, complete with lavish décor and an artificial stream flowing through the dining room, we dined on grilled lobster and beluga caviar on a riverbank terrace with a view of the fighting. A week later the restaurant was gone. Another Lon Nol officer with a secret dream to be a restaurateur, we concluded, had skipped out on his flailing country.

Plenty of the general's foot soldiers were worse than corrupt. They were absolute menaces to the population. Armed, drugged and mentally unhinged, the worst of them were deadly, not defensive, forces. I had a close encounter with one in a bakery one morning. I was paying for my baguette when a soldier, swaying and visibly impaired, entered. Instinctively I left without my change. Moments later the bakery exploded. The soldier had snapped and pulled the pin on his last grenade.

Meanwhile, I accepted in my own life an increasingly frightening duality. We worked and lived the best we could on the surreal stage of a warzone. We became numb to the danger and the carnage. We avoided the puddles of blood in the street and wrapped ourselves in wet sheets at night to fight the sweltering heat. I was, perhaps, better prepared for the physical endurance required from the experience than many. I had plenty of moments of despair, but there were others who broke down completely.

Though I never took for granted my capacity to endure the trials of Phnom Penh, I was no stoic. I, too, indulged in escapism. I was no stranger to Le Phnom, the down-at-the-heels luxury hotel where foreign correspondents gathered every night to expel the adrenaline of that day's junket out to a government-picked battlefield. Here, renowned journalists like Jon Swain and Al Rockoff, along with fellow Swedes, Herman Lindquist, Ole Tolgraven and Staffan Heimersson, shared a common *modus operandi* that we in the relief business were not immune to: *work hard, play harder.*

Drugs and alcohol were abundant. A local contingent of translators, fixers, and their enthusiastic female company helped mask the brief and twisted *dolce vita* of Phnom Penh on the edge of collapse. Many a night, the music at Le Phnom came close to drowning out the rocket fire from across the river. As 1974 ended and 1975 began, the party grew wilder. We knew the end was coming. In truth, we welcomed it. The resigned forces ostensibly defending the city were utterly discredited, and the advancing Khmer, it was nearly universally accepted, could only be an improvement.

We had no way of knowing that 1975 would not be the end of Phnom Penh's miserable siege. That instead, 1975 would become Year Zero.

By March the city was on a razor's edge. Nearly all the international NGO's had shuttered their offices and departures were daily among our aid community. We hung on the word of the senior UN official, a Swiss national by the name of Ferdinand Scheller, perhaps the only man in Phnom Penh who felt no urgency to leave. Outrageously optimistic and ever droll, Scheller always had a pithy explanation for our perseverance in English that was virtually unintelligible behind his walrus mustache. As the Resident Coordinator, Scheller's was the final word on the official UN presence in country. But he did not have the authority to force any employee to stay in Phnom Penh, which had now been classified as a Phase Four emergency – one in which, according to regulation understatement, "the security system has collapsed" and there was "no guarantee of safety," but which did not yet require the mandatory evacuation of a Phase Five emergency.

That said, we were all given the opportunity to relocate to Bangkok to wait out the imminent invasion of the Khmer Rouge, for we all fully believed that we would be able to operate on much more productive terms once the political limbo and inevitable attendant gunfire ceased. Kul Gautam was already there, working with the regional office on contingency plans. That left Ignatieff, Acar, Bjork, me, and all of our Cambodian staff, many of whom were now openly sympathetic to the rebels.

In mid-March, Wendy Bjork took up the offer to leave Phnom Penh. Paul Ignatieff asked me to accompany her, not because she required a chaperone, but because there was a cargo craft in Singapore whose crew refused to continue on to Phnom Penh's shattered airport without an international UN staffer to act as a human shield. I was to fly to Singapore via Bangkok and return with the much-needed cargo plane of supplies.

Wendy and I were offered seats out of the city on a C130 Hercules that had been dispatched from Canberra to evacuate the Australian Ambassador. We travelled in a convoy to the airport, which had changed hands multiple times in the preceding weeks but was in government control on that day. We waited for our aircraft in a sweltering bunker next to the ruined terminal. After several hours the plane arrived, and we scrambled aboard. The Ambassador's Mercedes Benz, its Australian flags fluttering gaily, was driven directly into the hold.

On the plane, Wendy, who had no intentions of setting foot in the god-forsaken country again, pulled out a sticky bottle of chartreuse liqueur and toasted the receding landscape. I accepted the bottle after her, knowing that I had a return flight that I'd rather not think about and saddened by the departure of one of our most dynamic co-workers, a woman whose charm and positive outlook had won over our local staff and would be sorely missed. Wendy and I passed that bottle for the rest of the forty-five minute flight and could hardly stand when we arrived in Bangkok.

The next morning I reported to the airport to accompany the Singapore based flight back to Cambodia and learned that the Khmer Rouge had retaken the airport. What's more, they had completely surrounded the capital. I would not be returning to Phnom Penh that day. Indeed, I would not be returning to Phnom Penh at all. I spent the next three weeks glued to the radio, following the events from afar.

In April, Lon Nol resigned. There was no government left in Cambodia. The American Embassy in Phnom Penh held a security briefing and invited the remaining international community. There was just one item to be briefed on: the Americans were leaving. The evacuation was open to all foreign nationals and any Cambodian who had been employed by American or other foreign organizations. The evacuation, Operation Eagle Pull, was scheduled for April 12.

About 300 people were airlifted from the city that day. None of them were my UNICEF colleagues, who, it was decided, would stay on and work for continuity through the Khmer Rouge takeover, which came five days later. Initially welcomed by the capital with cheers, white flags and even joy, the conquering rebels cut the euphoria short. Within days the new regime revealed its intentions. Scheller, Ignatieff and Acar, along with other foreigners and Cambodians of mixed ancestry or marriage, were arrested and incarcerated in the French consulate. The civilian population was given twenty-four hours to exit the city, from which they were escorted by forced march. Summary executions were the next horror. Anyone with eyeglasses, academic credentials, or ties to Western institutions was shot. Into this group fell the majority of our Cambodian UNICEF staff. The reign of "reeducation" and retribution had begun.

As untenable as the civilian agony of Phnom Penh seemed to us in the months before the Khmer Rouge seized power, what came afterwards was infinitely more agonizing. What came next was the slaughter of two million Cambodians by their own countrymen, the transformation of a beautiful, fertile, peaceful country into a concentration camp, and a scorched-earth policy to abolish the influences of western culture, scholarship, science and economic theory.

It took four years for the depths of the Khmer Rouge regime's depravity to be revealed, but just days for the international community to concede that we had gravely underestimated the potential for things to get worse and that we had seriously overestimated the good faith we had presumed the rebels would show the UN in response to our perseverance and willingness to work together.

About two weeks after the Khmer Rouge takeover, the last of Cambodia's foreign nationals, my colleagues among them, were trucked to the border in Aranyaprathet and released by grim-faced, black-clad rebels.

I was there to greet them. They were in reasonably good health but emotionally traumatized after two weeks of captivity and the threat of execution. As I embraced them and brooded over the fate of our Cambodian co-workers, I asked myself hard questions: *What was the point of our near impotent presence in Phnom Penh? Is there value in minimal effectiveness? Is it valuable enough to warrant the risks? Does the possibility of saving even one life justify risking the lives of would-be saviors?*

After thirty years knocking up against these same questions again and again, I have still not come to a satisfactory answer, nor have the UN statesmen and policy makers on whose decisions the lives of rank and file aid workers, peacekeepers, and civilian populations hang. Today's conflicts – whether the complex, multiparty militancy of DR Congo, the brazen defiance of international law in Syria, or the rise of such anti-west and anti-UN fanaticism as displayed by Al-Shabab, Boko Haram and ISIS – present risks and repercussions every bit as unfathomable and uncalculated as those of the Khmer Rouge. Moreover, the UN is a much larger target than it was in 1975; its employees are kidnapped, killed, and tortured regularly, and often in places where extreme insecurity and governmental dysfunction renders their presence symbolic, at best.

My conviction, stronger in hindsight, is that this symbolic force can be just as strong as a physical presence, particularly in conflict zones. For it is precisely when the UN leaves a troubled environment that the last hope is gone. This premise is true in many hellish arenas today where innocent lives are caught in the crossfire. Today, we consider the plight of hundreds and thousands of Syrians who are the victims, and sometimes hostages, of Bashar al-Assad. When the 300-person UN peacekeeping force departed from Damascus in August 2012, unable to justify its mission in the utter absence of a working peace accord, the international community despaired. What good, asked global skeptics, is the United Nations if it backs away from bullies who refuse to play by the rules of humanitarian law? They were right to ask. Yes, the mission had, up to that point, failed to minimize violence or to broker peace. What is worse, it had failed to secure the political will among the members of the Security Council to authorize it to keep working towards these goals. That, in my esteem, was its worst failure. When the UN pulls out of a troubled country it is sending the worst message: It is conceding a lost cause ... a terrible blow to those left behind, those whose sole cause is to survive.

In Phnom Penh in 1975, the distance between lost cause and lost hope was a matter of days. I believe that UNICEF gave as much to the people of Phnom Penh on the day it refused to leave the country in a US helicopter over the South China Sea as it did in all the months prior. But to this day I struggle with the basic dilemma of United Nations officials in conflict zones everywhere: At what cost do we give our commitment? And how do we tally the cost of hope when it is left in the dust of departing UN vehicles?

CHAPTER 5
Putting Phnom Penh Behind Me

FROM THE NIGHTMARE OF PHNOM PENH I was reassigned to Laos, another country tragically impacted by the tripartite power struggle that the United States, China and the Soviet Union had been inflicting on Southeast Asia for two decades.

There was no blood, no bombs and no marauding rebels on the streets of Vientiane, the Laotian capital. You could sleep at night, and you could make a plan for the week and usually stick to it. To be sure, the multi-ton influence of pugilists had been felt in the country in recent years– the US had flown thousands of bombing sorties over Laos in 1968 and 1969. But in 1975, the American presence was neutralized – there were several hundred USAID staff in residence when I arrived in April 1975, and the hi-octane party of jungle-hopping foreign correspondents and operatives had decamped from Le Phnom to the White Rose nightclub.

There was, nonetheless, a persistent tension in the city. Laos was the forgotten domino. The world's attention was on Vietnam and Cambodia and not on the Pathet Lao, a fringe group of Soviet-backed communist rebels beyond the urban centers who bore a striking resemblance to the Khmer Rouge of ten years earlier, albeit dressed in drab green rather than black. But if the outside world was distracted, the Laotians were not. A quiet exodus of the country's elite was already underway, and within six months of my arrival, the Pathet Lao was in the capital, and another domino had fallen.

The communist takeover in Laos was quiet but menacing. The Pathet Lao closed the borders and instituted a curfew, food rationing and constant surveillance. Individuals disappeared, whispered as threats to the revolution in need of "reeducation." This was a different sort of terror than that of the Khmer Rouge, employing a different method of psychological oppression. There was no merciless policy of internment and mass reprisal; but overnight Laos had become a police state. From then on, nightly summons were a reality, and re-education camps sprung up along the border with Vietnam.

The hedonism faded like mist. The bordellos, opium dens and nightclubs shut their doors, and the once-bustling boulevards looked like Main Street in a Wild Western ghost town. Cars were confiscated, and fuel was scarce; The American Ambassador travelled to work by rickshaw.

Worse was the heavy weight of suspicion. The Pathet Lao had infiltrated all of civil society to recruit informants. This was true even within our local staff, some of whom gave us cause for distrust. Meanwhile, in the corridors of the government, the expelled Americans made room for new expert advisors – consultants from the Eastern Bloc and Vietnam. On the streets, Laotians stringently avoided contact with westerners.

In late 1976 the Deputy Director of UNICEF, Charles Egger, and the head of UNICEF in Indochina, Jacques Beaumont, came to Laos to pay an official visit to the new regime and also to King Savang Vatthana, who remained the nominal monarch despite the communist takeover. The government agreed to allow our visit and provided us with a vintage DC2 to make the flight to Luang Prabang, the seat of the palace. We were informed that the King was too ill to receive us. We never did see him, and as a matter of fact, no one else did. He was never heard from again and declared dead of malaria in a re-education camp in 1978. Ours were the last names in the royal visitors' book.

My four years working with this regime were among the hardest in my career. As an international civil servant in a paranoid, isolated regime, I was compelled to work with officials who wanted our materials without our expertise, our strategies without our assistance, and our support without our suggestions. The Pathet Lao lacked an educated cadre to manage distribution, let alone governance, in the country. UNICEF was mandated to provide so-called "capacity support" for the regime to enable it to provide health, education and water and sanitation services to its youngest constituents. This was a significant endeavor in a state where skilled doctors and nurses had fled or had been removed from their positions and basic supplies were being hoarded. We had a responsibility to the population, but a presence contingent on the Pathet Lao's hospitality.

So we worked with the regime. Doing so meant, among other things, facilitating the purchase and delivery of printing presses so that the new government could produce new educational materials for state schools. We were, of course, aware that the new curriculum was decidedly ideological and that the textbooks we were financing would be used to indoctrinate young Laotians in the communist dogma that was now the ruling ideology of the country.

The only people in the office able to read the books we were printing were the Laotians, none of whom, I have to believe, had a greater loyalty to educational neutrality than they did to their personal safety. Moreover, in comparison with the much larger UNICEF office in Hanoi, which was under far more international and inter-agency scrutiny, our operation was a low priority. I don't know what discussions were taking place in the corridors of UNICEF's headquarters about producing propaganda in Laos, but I know how I personally justified it (when I took a break from cursing the obstacles to importing printing presses at all). I told myself that my ability to provide the populace with health and nutrition supplies was dependent on my willingness to also provide printing presses for propaganda. This willingness was complicity on one level, but more fundamentally, it was following orders as a junior UNICEF officer.

Increasingly, I engaged in unofficial, unsanctioned logistics, well beyond my professional responsibilities that, indeed, risked ruining my career. These were human logistics. Friends and colleagues came to me asking for assistance fleeing the country. I facilitated many nighttime crossings across the Mekong by canoe, totally unbeknownst to my employer, UNICEF, which could have been seriously implicated had my activities become known. Perhaps it was inevitable that after the traumatic inability to provide an exit from Cambodia's killing fields, I would do what I could to help people escape the oppressive regime in Laos. Most of them I have forgotten – their names and faces have receded with time. But there was one whose fate became permanently entwined with my own. Seng Pheth was a lovely girl who worked for the airlines and was immensely helpful to me in my work transporting supplies. She impressed me professionally, but also personally. When her father, a Brigadier General in the King's Army and a singularly upstanding patriot, was arrested and sentenced to the same reeducation camp that had become the final home of the King, I helped Seng Pheth flee the country. In the process, I fell in love with her. Our marriage, not long after the fall of Vientiane, was my personal happy ending to the domino theory.

Yes, Laos was an unhappy posting. But it gave me Seng Pheth, who, in turn, gave me two beautiful daughters, Christina and Linnéa. And for that I banish all my reservations about my unauthorized professional endeavors during those difficult years.

When I was transferred to Bangladesh in 1978, I was thrilled to leave the uneasiness of Vientiane behind. I was happier still to be able to give my new family a safe home in friendly country beyond the perimeter of ravaged Indochina. Adding to my satisfaction was the prospect of working in UNICEF's largest country office. The bureau in Dhaka enjoyed a full staff, an ample budget, long-term programming and operational normalcy. *What a relief,* I thought, envisioning a life free of urgency, uncertainty, and hardship. *I will have steady resources, an experienced staff, a daily routine without crises, and a measure of personal time.*

And I did, for about five months.

Then Henry Labouisse summoned me. Via telex, the UNICEF Executive Director directed me to join a scouting team to the Thai-Cambodia border. When I responded with a request for details, I was told that it was a "fact-finding mission," scheduled to take about two and a half weeks.

Those two and a half weeks turned into two and a half years. The task that emerged from that scouting mission – the protection of hundreds of thousands of Cambodians whom we had failed to protect four years earlier in Phnom Penh – was one I could not in good conscience refuse.

On the contrary, I welcomed the chance to redress that failing, despite my unhappiness at being away from my family – my youngest daughter had just been born.

That unusual, even extraordinary, event – a personal directive from the Executive Director to a low-level operative – put me in a predicament that many, many other international civil servants will recognize: My life as a humanitarian worker was on a collision course with my life as a family man. It was a collision that I successfully headed off, for better or worse, for fourteen years. But it could be felt as early as 1979 when I was called, once again, to Aranyaprathet on the Cambodian border.

CHAPTER 6
The Border Operation

Ever since the Khmer Rouge seized control of Cambodia, renaming it the Democratic Republic of Kampuchea and setting the clock at Year Zero, the regime had been fending off incursions by the Vietnamese. China and the USSR, the two superpowers left battling for hegemony in Asia, had leveraged the enmity of the two neighboring countries into a full-blown proxy war. Vietnam was the Soviets' dog in this fight, while China supported the more radically Maoist Khmer Rouge. Off the record but not entirely covertly, Thailand and the United States were also backing the Khmer Rouge despite the regime's evident terrorism against its own people. In the twisted logic of the Cold War, "the enemy of my enemy" (even if fanatically communist) was a de facto friend.

In December 1978, the Vietnamese launched a full invasion of Cambodia, toppling the government in January. The Khmer Rouge leadership retreated to the borderlands. Thai intelligence, the best source of information on movements in Cambodia, was spotty. It was generally believed that the Khmer Rouge in the countryside – overseers of an indoctrinated collectivized network of internal labor camps – had either abandoned their posts or were herding their civilian vassals ahead of the Vietnamese advance. The only certainty among the cables flying back and forth between New York, Bangkok, Geneva and Washington was that a massive human exodus was in the making. Thailand, always a key player in the delicate diplomacy of shifting alliances in Southeast Asia, was now ground zero for a developing humanitarian crisis. Dispatched by Henry Labouisse himself, I arrived back in Thailand just as the first visible wave of the exodus hit its eastern border in October 1979.

The traumatized human beings who emerged from the jungle that morning and altered the course of my career had been through a physical and emotional nightmare. They had been separated from their families, interred in labor camps, forced to work under deprivation, made to witness abuse and execution, and subjected to merciless psychological brainwashing and shocking physical violence. Society under the Khmer Rouge had been outlawed, and with it friendship, trust, romance and faith. Religion, money, and books were banned. Music and dance, the pride of the Khmer people, were corrupted to serve the anonymous, humorless, classless authority referred to collectively as "Angka."

Few knew the extent of this murderous legacy or of the utter decimation of the country that had sealed itself off from the world for more than four years. But the lack of life in the eyes of the women and children who had lived through this unfathomable nightmare gave us our first indication. By the time they reached the border, many of these survivors had traversed minefields, mass graves, and cordons of Khmer Rouge snipers and Vietnamese gunners.

The Thai emissary who accompanied me to the border to observe the arrival of the refugees had brought a Khmer translator. "Are there more of you?" he asked the dozen women who stood before us. They were silent. Not just wordless, but soundless - as if they had no more need of their voices. *Zombies*, was my first thought. *Zombies on earth*. I recalled a description that the journalist William Shawcross had shown me years before, a passage in a Pentagon report that described the Khmer as a "docile, passive people." This was not passivity, I knew. This was the destruction of will.

Then one of them, a young woman, broke the silence with a short sound of affirmation. She lifted her hand in a gesture of explanation and then turned back to the jungle. We followed her into the sweltering canopy of trees. Within half a kilometer we were surrounded by the prone figures of the dead and dying. There were hundreds of them. And there were thousands more within a day's journey.

Once we had communicated the urgency of the situation to our respective superiors through the proper channels, the resources were quick to follow. The small community of aid workers in the vicinity scrambled into a crisis brigade. Our initial objective was simply to keep people alive. I used my first cash disbursement from the UNICEF regional office in Bangkok to buy every mattress and hire every flatbed truck in the Aranyaprathet vicinity. We commandeered the local health clinic and asked the International Federation of Red Cross and Red Crescent Societies and the NGO community to send as many medical professionals as possible to the border. We set up makeshift shelters of bamboo. We dug burial pits.

Twenty-four hours later we were still ferrying bodies, administering life-saving hydration and triage, and digging graves. There were now eight to ten thousand people camped on the border. Two weeks later, they numbered 470,000. The rainy season had begun, making the lack of solid shelters, latrines, and roads critical. We were still in disaster containment mode, but I knew that the time was coming when the operation would need to drop its *ad hoc* nature and secure leadership, organization and legitimacy.

I tried not to think of what formalization entailed: the negotiations of myriad parties, few of whom put human lives at a priority. Geopolitical wrangling, of course, was already at work. I knew that it would soon rear its ugly head right here at the border and make our work infinitely more complicated. But the intrusion was inevitable. The situation on the Thai-Cambodia line was an unprecedented emergency unfolding in the middle of a geopolitical hornet's nest. There was no avoiding the stings.

Our early census pointed at the root of all our problems to come: the wave of refugees had brought with it the detritus of an entire country in upheaval. For every ten innocent children and suffering mothers in our makeshift camp, there was a handful of Khmer Rouge, ranging from active militants to former commandants to low-level party opportunists. For every man that stepped forward to volunteer responsibility for a segment of the refugee population, there was another who saw the operation as a path towards enrichment. In short, there was little chance of maintaining a purely humanitarian operation. The presence of Khmer refugees on the border was a geopolitical event, and the civilians sheltering there were seen alternately as pawns, buffers, human shields or camouflage for the war criminals in their midst.

With the Thai military willfully blind to the activities of a loose confederation of "liberators" on its doorstep, much of the border was a no-man's land. In the naturally fortified northern and southern sections, armed factions were given free reign to set up bases from which to launch a counter-attack on the Vietnamese. The central section, a wide, unprotected plain north and south of Aranyaprathet, became the clearest path for the flood of refugees. The Thai government knew they could not be ignored, despite the very evident presence of militants and warlords in their midst. On the contrary, Bangkok would soon value the refugee population as a human buffer against Vietnamese expansion.

The refugee megapolis that formed on the border in late 1979 was as self-contained as it was utterly dependent on foreign aid. Because so many of the refugees arrived in groups either protected, chaperoned or simply conscripted into larger factions, this central border organized itself into loose political alignments.

Mak Moun camp, the largest, was nominally the camp of the Khmer Serai, or "Free Khmer," who sought to overthrow both the Khmer Rouge and the occupying Vietnamese. It was a rough environment, a squalid shantytown of as many as 250,000 souls, led by an odious bandit named Van Seran whose intended "liberation" of his motherland was a blatantly cynical masquerade. Nearby, Phnom Chat, Nong Pru and Ta Prik were Khmer Rouge enclaves, though their camp leaders did not always identify themselves as such. A third faction, loyalists of Prince Sihanouk, ran the Nong Chan and Nong Samet camps. Here, the leaders made an effort to isolate women and children from the militants, making them by far the safest and least criminal of the camps.

These were the people I was tasked with protecting – some 500,000 traumatized Cambodians still trapped by the agendas of the armed minority in their midst. Having lived for so long with no other rule of law than the threat of death, they largely accepted the authority of their self-proclaimed leaders. The presence of these militants, welcomed by our Thai hosts but abhorred by the Vietnamese-installed regime in Phnom Penh, made our task of supporting the largest population of Khmer outside Cambodia the target of international criticism. Worse, politics sometimes caused real vulnerability for the refugees, already exposed to internal violence, disease and exploitation.

Thailand, ostensibly committed to an "open door" policy for the refugees, nonetheless insisted that they be confined to the border region. Only two holding centers, established before the refugee flood were permitted. They were maintained by UNHCR, the UN High Commissioner for Refugees. Sa Kaeo camp was established for Khmer Rouge refugees. Khao I Dang was for non Khmer Rouge refugees.

As for the hundreds and thousands halted at the border, UNHCR denied all responsibility, proclaiming that civilians located fewer than six kilometers from their national borders did not qualify as refugees, but as "internally displaced people." This was a concept that would change in a matter of years, as more and more people found themselves made homeless within their own country; But in Vietnamese-occupied Cambodia, UNHCR pointed to this limbo status as a pretext for not providing assistance. It was Henry Labouisse who determined that UNICEF would not shirk this responsibility. And so I found myself at the head of the agency's largest refugee camp since World War II.

Meanwhile, Hanoi recognized the displaced Khmer as a convenient cloak for the enemy that had not yet been routed. As such, the Vietnamese army carried out daily raids and bombings of the densely populated border in a bid to flush out guerillas. UNICEF, the provider of last resort on the border, was the lead agency in an operation that defied all objectives of neutrality.

The authority of UN relief workers in the region was further eroded by the political sparring within the Security Council itself over the contested seat of Cambodia in the General Assembly. China would not allow the new regime to replace the Khmer Rouge as the UN voice of the Khmer people. Equally unhelpful was the fact that UNICEF, having succeeded in re-opening the office in Phnom Penh, had to be careful not to anger the new Vietnamese-installed government, even as the agency's executive director was actively volunteering UNICEF to provide for the displaced people that UNHCR had determined were not "refugees."

In the end, the orders came from the very top: UN Secretary General Kurt Waldheim authorized the Khmer Border Relief as an UNICEF-coordinated operation, allowing me, my team, and our International Committee of the Red Cross partners (ICRC) to step boldly from out of our semi-covert shadows. With our reputation preceding us, UNICEF and ICRC were permitted to act on purely humanitarian grounds, blind and deaf to the endless debates at the UN. The World Food Programme joined us by providing food aid. But the UNICEF/ICRC joint-operation camps, taking on every complexity of the military, political and diplomatic environments surrounding them, remained controversial.

This attendant criticism, negotiations, compromise and diplomacy was no more than a distracting buzz in my ears throughout 1979, as I struggled with my team to save lives and to accommodate the flood of refugees from my new base in Aranyaprathet. I kept my focus and applied pressure where I knew it would be acknowledged. When Henry Labouisse asked me how many personnel I needed, I told him a minimum of 120 staff. I heard the Executive Director gasp slightly. In an era when emergency relief had not yet become the global industry that it is today, this was a significant request. UNICEF simply did not have 120 spare field officers available, particularly ones with emergency experience. Not a man for cursing, Labouisse wondered, "Where the hell am I going to find you 120 volunteers?" I told him I didn't know, but I was hiring able-bodied Thai men and women from Bangkok and out of the local market and anywhere I could find them.

Not long after this discussion, my volunteers began arriving from the New York headquarters. They were administrators, technicians, and even some secretaries. I learned later that they had all been recruited by a personal plea for volunteers signed by Labouisse and posted in the canteen. This is how I wound up with five secretaries who had scarcely left the boroughs of New York City suddenly facilitating operations in a dangerous, crowded, highly fragile refugee camp. They thought it would be an adventure; and it was. They were among the hardest workers I had on the border, and after their three-month gig they did not want to go home. I credited them with a boundless enthusiasm and ability to weather difficult conditions. But I also credited my old boss, Paul Ignatieff, who had taught me how to get on the right foot with your staff. I picked up every new volunteer and officer from the local airstrip myself. And every Saturday night I held a potluck dinner at my house. I kept these practices sacred throughout my career, in every duty station I served. Because in all countries, climates and crises, morale was always in need of bolstering.

Labouisse and his deputy, Charles Egger, remained my most responsive supporters, coming regularly to the border to observe the operation not long after we were up and running. I took the opportunity to let him know that we were still strapped for vehicles. Because the Thai government feared potential permanence of a half million Cambodians on their border (a fear that was not at all unwarranted), the seven camps in my purview all lacked basic infrastructure, including decent roads to join them. "During the monsoons I am trying to cross rivers in a Suzuki the size of your office sofa," I told him. Labouisse considered this and then turned to look at the car that had brought him out to the border. It was a Toyota Crown, an ambassadorial sedan that belonged to the Regional Director. "Will that one do for now?" he asked.

And so I began making my rounds in a car that, if not entirely fit for a monsoon, did lift my credibility for a bit. In time, UNICEF secured a fleet of 140 cars for my team on the border. By then, the UNICEF/ICRC joint-operation employed 5,000 aid workers (most of the Cambodian refugees themselves) along with hundreds of foreign workers from international NGO's, joining my grass-roots troops of about 200 Thai workers. We were fielding convoys of up to 80 vehicles a day, distributing a half million liters of water and hundreds of tons of rice over a 100 kilometer range from Aranyaprathet.

But still we were under-resourced. This, again, was a legacy of geopolitical compromise. While we struggled to provide rudimentary aide to half a million people, the UNHCR transit center twelve kilometers away in Khao I Dang, was a virtual paradise. This camp housed just Cambodian refugees who were eligible for third-country resettlement, and it was worlds away from the reality in the UNICEF/ICRC border camps: In Khao I Dang, residents attended schools, worshipped in temples, got married and celebrated birthdays; In our camps, inhabitants were shelled by the Vietnamese. Journalists and visiting dignitaries (my Swedish King and

Queen included) were taken to Khao I Dang; The only visitors to our camps were the Khmer Rouge guerillas looking for supplies and soldiers.

We were aware of their presence. Even the non-Khmer Rouge camps of Mak Moun and Nong Chan were infiltrated by black marketers and bristling with guns. Given the mandate to protect women and children, UNICEF lacked the means to enforce protection. Ostensibly under Thai martial law, the camps were ruled internally. The Thai army had orders to turn a blind eye, and, we were fairly certain, in some instances to supply both the Khmer Rouge and the right wing rebel group, Khmer Serai, to continue fighting the Vietnamese army. On many occasions I went head to head with the leader of Mak Moun, Van Seran, who insisted on taking full control of food distribution in the massive camp. Knowing that nearly three-quarters of the disbursements were being funneled back out of the camp, I alternately refused, negotiated and fumed. Once I turned the food trucks around, still fully loaded, because Van Seran had brought his soldiers to commandeer the cargo. He told me I could expect to pay for my intransigence with my life. Not long afterwards a grenade landed in my living room. Happily, it failed to detonate.

The gangster Van Seran plagued me for months, until finally the Thai military decided he was as troublesome to the state as he was to my operations. One night, well after the curfew that banned my staff and me from the camps, armed soldiers raided Mak Moun and herded all of its occupants to other refugee centers inside the border. Van Seran disappeared and never troubled me again, but the knowledge that the Thai army could act unilaterally, without much consideration for the refugee population, was a source of wariness for as long as I remained on the border.

It was a delicate balance - standing on principal and getting results. I became quite good at bush diplomacy, the first lesson of which is knowing precisely your strengths and your weaknesses. In his book "The Quality of Mercy," the British journalist William Shawcross gave me the title "Baron of the Border," but I was perfectly aware that my power – food, water and sanctuary – was far from uncontested. I remember the first time I refused to send food distributions into a camp whose 'security' team was found re-selling our rice on the black market. I remember laying down criteria for deliveries to Khmer Rouge-controlled camps and chafing under direct orders to recommence such deliveries. I remember the discussions about diverting trucks to feed Thai villagers whose poverty made them covetous of the World Food Programme rations in our convoys. I remember the night I accepted the universal truth that soldiers eat first, men eat second, and women and children last. That acceptance became the basis of my border logic and remained a tenant of the *realpolitik* with which I approached many more humanitarian operations to come. It is patently unfair, of course, this truth. But it is the one that would have to rule my disbursements as well if I did not want more deaths on my hands.

Still, there were days when we went into huts and removed sacks of rice. There were nights we heard gunshots after curfew that signaled those sacks had been confiscated once more. I lost sleep over my knowledge that our food rations were feeding combatants and corruption. In the most discouraging weeks, we saw women who had patiently endured brazen theft and other grievances finally snap; One day, those long-suffering women all but destroyed one of our trucks in a stampede. My staff carried out nutritional surveys and instituted women-only delivery days to ensure that the neediest were provided for, but I knew that I had an equal responsibility to my dauntless staff, and so I had to accept that there was a natural distribution of resources that was beyond my ability to control.

And so we continued our operations in brutal, substandard conditions under curfew and bombardment and relentless criticism. We worked from sunup to sundown and then retired to Aranyaprathet. The camps, armed as any inner city and as dangerous as any impoverished slum, were off-limits after dark. For my staff I held weekend dinners and insisted on frequent R&R. And I advised them that to avoid making their blood boil, they should stay away from Khao I Dang, which flaunted the disparity between two UN agencies ostensibly working for the same cause – humanity. The UNHCR's "border Hilton" was salt in the wound left by the UN's divisiveness over the fate of the disenfranchised refugees.

While the Thai authorities took international credit for the excellent conditions at Khao I Dang in Thai territory, they were intransigent about providing the border camps with the sort of infrastructure that might encourage permanence. That meant no paved roads, no permanent structures, no latrines or drilled wells. Not a single bag of concrete was permitted in our camps, lest the refugees decide to colonize the border. We made do within these paranoid conditions until two minor crises collided to create a major emergency.

The first was the outbreak of cholera in Long Chan camp, a serious situation in any case. We had just managed to get the highly transmissible disease more or less under control when Colonel Prachak Sawaengchit, head of the Thai military security division on the border, announced that he was putting the camp under a supply embargo as punishment for a skirmish between one of his own men and a rebel Khmer Rouge soldier in the camp. I knew that without daily water supplies, the cholera would spread rapidly out of control. Hat in hand I made my way to Prachak's office. He was a loathsome man, renowned for his offensive self-importance and crass behavior, and we had sparred before over our respective authorities. But I was prepared to tolerate his inflated tales of valor during the Vietnam War and enumeration of Vietcong he had killed to secure my precious water deliveries. Instead, I got an earful of his bluster combined with a vehement denial of my request. Prachak made it clear that he considered my solicitation on behalf of the camp a challenge to his iron fist.

Vaguely disgusted but not defeated, I took my case next to a levelheaded, high-minded man named Kitty, who served as the civilian administrator of the border zone under martial law. Like Prachak, Colonel Kitty was a veteran of the Vietnam War, a black beret and Special Forces commander, but he had none of his counterpart's brutal bluster. On the contrary, Kitty's genuine generosity towards the plight of the refugees put us on great terms and helped us see eye to eye. It was Kitty who would take the time to inform me of nighttime incidents in the camp and even accompany me during curfew so that I could begin immediate damage control.

When Kitty heard my version of events, he promised to intercede with Prachak on my behalf. In the meantime, he advised me that I was to proceed with deliveries, but discreetly. We did so, at four o'clock in the morning. The camp's residents hurried to meet me with the startling request that I vacate the camp immediately. They feared the wrath of Colonel Prachak more than they feared the deadly disease in their midst. I honored their wishes, but only after I had emptied my truck.

Again following Kitty's advice, I made myself scarce for the next several days. I found a pretext to be in Bangkok and out of Prachak's reach. But the moment I returned to the border, there was no avoiding a showdown. I was summoned to Prachak's jungle bunker. I drove myself and was met by the Colonel brandishing a gun. He reeked of cognac, and he raged about my insubordination. Then he put the pistol to my head and rasped, "I have shot men for lesser things. You made me lose face."

I understood the gravity of the situation. In Thailand, and in much of Asia, "losing face," is a fate worse than cholera. Particularly if you are a testosterone-driven despot like Prachak. I appealed to his medals, his gun, and his code of honor. I dredged up my military training. "I have never in my life committed an act of insubordination," I promised him. "I am a soldier like you. But I have my own orders. My duty is to fulfill the commands of my superiors and to provide water for the inhabitants of all camps under the UNICEF Border Operation. Not to do so would be a dereliction of my duty."

To my great surprise, Colonel Prachak invited me, a fellow soldier, to lunch. After sharing a glass of cognac and securing the Colonel's assurance that he would reassess the embargo, I extricated myself. I drove the long way back to Aranyaprathet with my hands trembling. In part, I was still unnerved by the gun to my head, but mostly I was shaking with rage. *How dare that man threaten an international civil servant? How dare he make innocent women and children hostage to his own self-importance?* In my anger, I considered reporting the incident and making Prachak, a loose cannon, into the target of an international inquiry. Luckily, the drive was long enough for me to take that scenario to its logical conclusion: Prachak the war veteran would survive, emboldened and with his face secure. I, a junior programme officer whose present responsibilities vastly outpaced my formal rank and organizational visibility, would be removed from my post.

Cooler heads prevailed. In time I learned to engage in "cognac diplomacy" with this particularly rough interlocutor. At any rate, I did not have to suffer him much longer. Prachak was at the head of a failed coup against the government in Bangkok. He was arrested and jailed for treason in 1981. After his release, he committed suicide. The news of his death conjured up unpleasant memories, but also some remorse. Prachak and I had found a very small patch of common ground as soldiers and sharers of a snifter or three of cognac.

By November 1979 the refugee crisis on the border was global news. Sadly, the world was not getting the full picture. Visiting dignitaries and reporters were regularly diverted to that model refuge, Khao I Dang. The First Lady of the United States, Rosalynn Carter, visited Sa Keo camp in the territory of Thailand, posed with a small child, urged authorities to improve the conditions in camp, and caught the next flight out.

I jumped and hollered and waved my hands, but the Thai authorities argued that they could not guarantee the safety of foreigners on the border. More to the point, they did not want the world to see the misery of the hundreds of thousands of Khmer just across the dividing line lest they be compelled to take more of them into the safer sanctuary of their sovereign territory. While we were indebted to Thailand for allowing us to work on its territory, we were also conscious that our presence was a reliable human buffer for Bangkok against Vietnam and Hanoi's suspected expansionist goals.

Some journalists managed to flout the security protocols and to find their way to the border where they helped convey the enormity of the crisis. Also critical to communicating the situation was the NGO community, which was growing rapidly at that time. Born out of the horrors of the 1971 Biafran crisis and schooled in the challenges of the Ethiopian famine of 1973, countless non-governmental organizations saw Aranyaprathet as their next great *raison d'être*.

At their best, these organizations contributed hugely to the refugee response: Care, led by a dynamic American named Tom Alcedo; Irish Concern, founded by the brothers Gus and Jck Finucain; as well as World Vision, CRS and many others emerged as highly respected players in the theater of international relief work. But a small number of newly created NGOs were symptomatic of the world's response to the crisis: an outpouring of sympathy misdirected towards ineffective projects. At one point, the UNICEF warehouse was the end depot for three cargo planes full of utterly useless "supplies" including long johns and expired vitamins donated by an American NGO. When we ran out of space in our warehouse for the potato chips and sunglasses from this well-meaning donor, we dug a pit in the ground and buried them. The sympathy of the American public was commendable. Their awareness of the conditions we faced was less so.

The funding for the border operation came primarily from the governments of Australia, the UK, Japan, Germany, the Nordic countries and the United States. (Washington contributed about half of the total foreign aid to our operation.) After these a very important contribution came from the government of Italy. Because Cambodia had been thoroughly mined first by the Khmer Rouge and then by the Vietnamese, we were in urgent need of a surgeon who could perform amputations on hundreds of maimed victims. Dr. Guido Bertolaso arrived in early 1980 with a highly professional team of surgeons that was operating within days. Though their task was grim, the surgeons we called "bone crackers" were a joyful infusion for our team. They had come well equipped for their mission: They brought state of the art medical equipment and not one, but two chefs. The best spaghetti puttanesca I ever ate was served outside the surgery of Aranyaprathet. Bertolaso, with his inexhaustible good-humor and positive attitude, was an asset in his own right. About a decade after he left the Cambodian operation, he became the Deputy Executive Director of UNICEF and later still, the head of Italy's Department of civil defense.

WITHIN OUR COMMUNITY on the border, I relied on many remarkable colleagues, though I didn't always immediately appreciate their presence. For example – the confident young Brit who appeared at my office in clothes better suited for High Street than for the border who took one look at my grubby clothes and asked for the officer in charge. I gave him the requisite response, which something like "I am. And who the hell are you?" His name, he managed in apology to my gruff welcome, was Mark Malloch Brown, and we went on to become close friends and colleagues. I greatly admired the cheeky young representative of the UN High Commissioner for Refugees (UNHCR), who is today an actual baron and decorated international civil servant. I was not a bit surprised when he became the Deputy Secretary General of the United Nations under Kofi Annan. If he weren't effectively ruled out as a citizen of a country that has a permanent member of the Security Council, I would support Malloch Brown's candidacy for Secretary General.

It was also during my border responsibilities that I first met Sergio Viera de Mello, a handsome and charismatic Brazilian working, like Brown, for UNHCR. I met with de Mello in Bangkok several times and would cross his path again later when I joined the High Commissioner's staff in 1991. Sergio's integrity, passion and charm made him a favorite inside and outside the UN. In 2003, less than a year after appointing him High Commissioner on Human Rights, Secretary General Kofi Annan persuaded Sergio to take a temporary post as the Special Representative in Baghdad. Personally requested by US President George W. Bush, it proved to be Sergio's last appointment. On August 19, 2003, a suicide bomb at the Canal Hotel in Baghdad killed Sergio and twenty-two others. A second bombing less than a month later prompted the withdrawal of nearly all six-hundred people staffing the United Nations Assistance Mission in Iraq.

It was a pivotal moment in UN history. Critics were outraged that the UN had been used by the United States to legitimize an illegitimate war. More than a decade later, you can hear the echoes of the debate among US policy-makers. With Iraq once again in a state of anarchy, some blame George Bush for starting a destabilizing war, while others blame Barack Obama for a premature withdrawal. But most agree that the United Nations must show more caution in the region.

I have learned to be careful with blame. When I look at the tragedy of the Canal Hotel, I see the rock and the hard place between which the UN is so often squeezed. I see a battleground where innocent civilians deserve the normalcy that the presence of the United Nations can provide, and I also see the message of despair that the UN sent the people of Iraq when it retreated from intolerably high losses.

But if Sergio Viera de Mello's death represents for many observers the UN's naïveté and vulnerability in Iraq, his life represents, for me, a breadth of understanding and depth of compassion that we should all strive to emulate. Long after we met in Thailand, I worked closely with Sergio to resolve lingering tensions in the aftermath of genocide in Burundi. More personally, he was a source of enormous support when I suffered my own loss in that country. I have held him as a model ever since.

Another of my border angels was Sami Behran, a mechanic. He was a low-level officer sent out by UNICEF from Bangladesh, but his immense natural talent for problem solving was immediately apparent, and I made him my logistics chief. Sami was a quiet man who spoke six languages but said little. As an Egyptian Copt and the adopted son of a Danish couple, he counted Amarinya, Danish and Hebrew as his mother tongues. He was an absolute wizard at surmounting obstacles. As long as the problem affected inventory in the warehouse, Sami would tackle the problem calmly, the smoke of his ever-present cigarette wreathing his head like the solution he was concocting.

Equally invaluable was his crack-team of garage overseers, Boon and Tiew. These two women were college graduates who had come out from Bangkok looking for a challenging first job. Sami put them to work negotiating rates with our relief truck drivers. To my astonishment, the petite pair proved to be dogged and shrewd, their good looks and traditional docile demeanor completely belying their take-no-hostages negotiation skills and take-no-nonsense rebuffs of the rowdy truck drivers. I was equally impressed by the Thai college students who volunteered their services as food monitors in the camp. They took their jobs as early identifiers of child malnutrition in the camps very seriously and never complained about the heat or monsoon rains that accompanied them on their daily rounds.

Throughout my assignment in Aranyaprathet, I was always aware of how much more there was to learn as a UNICEF Representative of the Kampuchean Border Operation. I looked to Robert Jackson as a mentor. The man known to most as "Jacko" was a legendary figure: the recipient of a Knight Bachelor, a Hero of Malta, and the leader of the Murmansk Convoy. Jacko and I met in January 1981. His trip to Aranyaprathet, specifically to see me was a refreshing gesture of respect from one so high-ranking, and we discussed every element of my authority including staffing needs, warehouse capacity, transport contingencies, and the universal under-appreciation of trial-and-error.

As the Secretary General's Special Represenitive for the Cambodian operation, he was indispensable in helping navigate the continuous gridlock and outright hostility between UNICEF's Phnom Penh and border operations. In two and half years on the border, I never had direct talks with my colleagues in Phnom Penh, but Jacko helped smooth issues that needed our cooperation. Leagues ahead of me in rank and stature, Sir Jackson always treated me as an equal and imparted invaluable wisdom, such as his parting message to me: "You will assemble many acquaintances over the years, but if you have, at the end of it all, just a handful of friends, real friends, then you will be a rich man."

All in all, my staff and coworkers on the border embodied the best of humanitarian compassion, technical know-how and determination to make the best of a rough situation. Their personal and professional commitment was put into sharp relief when displayed alongside that of Kurt Waldheim, the world's highest-ranking international civil servant. Waldheim, the Secretary General of the United Nations, flew to Aranyaprathet in May 1980 with his deputy, Perez de Cuellar. He had stopped over in Phnom Penh for talks with some of the entities (my UNICEF colleagues included) most opposed to our oeration on the border. We had planned to win him over with that most guileless of means: singing children and welcome banners. But Secretary Waldheim arrived in a foul mood, having slammed his toe in a hotel lobby. Ten minutes into our ceremony, he left. I was mortified before the confused refugees. I could discourse at length over the shortcomings of that man, the UN's fourth Secretary General, but there's no need. History has already written the man's epitaph. Suffice it to say that the day the Secretary General left refugee children to perform without an audience was not the United Nations' finest hour.

But I had already experienced many fine hours.

CHAPTER 7

The Land Bridge

AS THE YEAR 1980 DREW TO A CLOSE and the emergency operation in Aranyaprathet fell into something resembling normalcy (distributions were regular and nearly as predictable as Vietnamese bombardments and diplomatic stalemates), the sense of urgency shifted from the border to Cambodia's interior. The human exodus from the fertile plateaus had resulted in a domestic food shortage. While there was no shortage of international food aid being flown into Phnom Penh, the government was proving incapable - or perhaps unwilling - to distribute it to the starving population. The threat of famine loomed.

With our own distributions becoming systematic, if still imperfect, we began to consider the problem of extending aid back into the country, if for no other reason than to encourage the refugees to move towards a future resettlement. The American ambassador to Thailand, a dynamic and pragmatic man named Morton Abramowitz, was in negotiations with Bangkok to rehabilitate transportation over the border and into Cambodia, but the Vietnamese puppet government balked at American involvement.

In December we learned that negotiations to reopen the road or railway had broken down irrevocably. And so the oft-raised possibility of a "land bridge" to feed the country from the outside in became the best option. The fluidity on the border, where many peasants who didn't live in the camps found them to be an excellent source of food, would serve a double purpose. These peasant commuters, with their oxcarts and unwillingness to become permanent refugees, could help replant the rice paddies and feed the hungry Cambodians left in the collapsed nation. In fact, they had already begun.

The programme began informally. One day we simply handed over 100 five-kilo bags of rice to a handful of farmers at Nong Chan. We told them if they came back in a week, we would have other supplies for them: seed, fishing nets, farm implements and fertilizer.

Such supplies were not in UNICEF's usual catalog of relief items. Initially, headquarters was skeptical. There were those who objected, reflexively, to the notion that aid was being diverted from our officially mandated constituency – the inhabitants of the UNICEF/ICRC joint-operation camps. But I explained the logic of helping rehabilitate the interior and, ultimately, civil society in Cambodia. This argument won out.

Robert Ashe was a British aid worker with Christian Outreach, who helped refine the logistical end of the operation into a major distribution system. We consulted with Khmer elders and villagers about the best way to avoid confiscation of the supplies. Their input helped minimize diversions and siphoning. Passed on entirely by word of mouth, the schedule of land bridge disbursements nonetheless proceeded with more order and regularity than many of our camp distributions. The logistics were intricate and necessitated a ration system to reserve supplies for these commuters, separate from the camp inhabitants.

Watching the weekly land bridge in action was spectacularly cinematic: an enormous armada of ox-carts, hundreds and sometimes thousands strong, cresting waves of dust at day-break as they approached the border at Nong Chan. Sometimes they arrived the night before, in which case we were alerted by the pleasant chorus of a thousand lowing oxen. Regardless of the time, their arrival always made me euphoric. It was such a welcome sight, following that first parade of misery to the border and countless hardships and failures in between.

In time, the weekly distribution transferred 250,000 tons of food and 10,000 tons of seed and fertilizer, as well as tools and fishing nets, back into Cambodia. We estimated that a kilo of seed could provide a family for one year inside Cambodia. Ambassador Abramowitz, who continued to be a great support to us, credited the land bridge with averting famine the following year.

Just as importantly, we sensed that the participants in our efforts – the 'captains' of our land bridge – farmers who waited for hours in the sweltering sun for their allotment, were also there to accept ownership over their country and to take back the very resources that had been stripped from them by forced collectivization. We imagined that the tilling of the soil far from the border was therapeutic for land and tiller both. The men and women who travelled the land bridge were grateful, informative and patient in their interactions with us. Their regard was a refreshing change from our frequent sparring with camp warlords. We learned about conditions inside the country from them, and to this day I count dozens of beautifully engraved oxen-yokes, gifts from the farmers of the land bridge, among my prized souvenirs. Watching them trundle back to their fallow fields, their carts filled with Cambodia's future, was a profound sight. It was only a matter of time before the camp refugees, equally inspired, began to follow in their tracks, pioneers of the land bridge home.

For those who were unable or still unwilling to return home, we tried to provide meaning and activity beyond the ennui and deprivation of refugee life. We were painfully aware that they were double victims – victims of terror in their homeland and later, victims of a political standoff between the UN and the new government. This protracted challenge made even our small victories bittersweet.

When we were finally granted permission to construct of a temple in Mak Moun camp, for example, the impact on morale was so noticeable that the Thai authorities softened their stance against permanent structures and gave the green light for schools, gardens and even a clinic. At the time, these were very real causes for celebration, improving daily life on the border for thousands. Not for one moment did we hesitate over the wisdom of introducing such small comforts to the border. But then we never considered the possibility that the miserable camps that we established in late 1979 out of utter humanitarian necessity would become, due to intransigent internal UN divisiveness, home to thousands of refugees for fourteen more years.

One year after I began my assignment in Aranyaprathet, in October 1980, I traveled to UNICEF headquarters in New York to report on our activities. When I attended a gathering in the UN Economic and Social Council, I was stunned to find that my own colleagues, UNICEF staff from Phnom Penh with whom I had never had direct contact, refused to recognize me or to hold a discussion with me. Absorbed with their own difficulties in working with the paranoid puppet government installed by Vietnam, they had conflated Hanoi's enemies – the Khmer Rouge – with the refugees that I was responsible for providing for. They looked at me if not as a foe to the Khmer people, than certainly as an obstacle to their in-country programme.

By then, other international watchdogs had taken firmly in their teeth the issue of Khmer Rouge indemnity (an admittedly valid proposition to which our border operation was vulnerable). Their allegations that UNICEF supplies were going to war criminals and architects of genocide shook me as much as my colleague's deliberate snub. I argued the case of humanity, of the rules of the jungle that would never treat women and children fairly and that therefore had to be subverted with bush diplomacy. I stood my ground in the hallways of the General Assembly, firm in my belief that the United Nations, an organization committed to the fair and equitable and peaceful rapport of nations, had allowed the Khmer Rouge to remain in Cambodia's chair and speak for Cambodia's people, and therefore I, like all UN servants, had to respect the voice of the Khmer Rouge. It was a morally fraught decision, but it was not mine to bear alone. On the contrary, I faced my own demons daily when I negotiated with Khmer Rouge and non-Khmer Rouge chieftains to get food and supplies to women and children. My job was to negotiate with the forces that both helped and hindered my humanitarian objective. My job was to serve the people on the border at Aranyaprathet who couldn't hear a damn thing that was said in the Security Council or the General Assembly or the Economic and Social Council. But those were conversations I had outside the chamber and sometimes just in my head.

At the close of the meetings, Tommy Koh, Singapore's representative to the UN and a key participant in the rancorous debates over Cambodia's representation in the UN, took the podium to denounce the presence of the Khmer Rouge representative. He did not mince words, and I did not disagree with him. But I despaired that Koh's passionate judgment would do nothing to help the Khmer whose fates hung in the balance on the Thai border. I knew that Koh shared my hope that the refugees could soon be repatriated by a responsible state under international observation. Then Koh paused and cleared his throat. When he spoke again, his voice had a different tone entirely.

"I would now like to recognize one of the heroes of the Khmer," he said. And to my great astonishment and gratification, the delegates took a moment out of its self-inflicted agony over choosing the lesser of two evils as the voice of the suffering Khmer people, to applaud the efforts of a much maligned project to prioritize humanity over unanimity. I rose and accepted the recognition of the UNICEF Khmer Border operation on behalf of my team and the struggling families outside Aranyaprathet.

THE CAMBODIAN REFUGEE CRISIS showed the United Nations at its very best and at its very worst. If the mass murder of two million Khmers was the fault of an insidious fanatical faction, the long displacement of one million more waslargely the result of the UN's impotence to enforce moral reparation for that crime.

In the years following Vietnam's installation of a puppet regime, the UN repeatedly tripped over its own democratic feet. The Security Council became a boxing ring, where rival super-powers China and the United States ganged up to deliver the knock-out punch to the Soviet-backed, Vietnamese-installed government that had replaced the Khmer Rouge in Phnom Penh but, without international recognition, could not speak for Cambodia on the world stage. In this political battle, concern for hundreds of thousands of men, women and children was hijacked by politics. Often the debate took on moral righteousness – the atrocities of the Khmer Rouge regime made for a powerful argument ... but not powerful enough to install a government with enemies in the Security Council. And so the Khmer Rouge kept the seat in the General Assembly. The debacle of an emasculated, discredited, and deeply tainted entity representing the people of Cambodia for more than a decade after the killing fields showed the UN at its worst.

Righting human wrongs is not a quick process and justice has come slowly to Cambodia. Earlier this year, a tribunal sentenced two of the top leaders of the Khmer Rouge to life in prison. They are very old men now – Khieu Samphan and Nuon Chea. But I rejoice, nonetheless, that justice has been served in a UN-backed court, no matter how belatedly.

Our work on the border, on the other hand, represented the UN at its best and its most timely. Removed but not insulated from the political debate that our operation generated, the UNICEF Khmer border relief was immediate and effective, saving countless lives. The remarkable land bridge that generated from our operation helped the country mend. Isolated as we were from Bangkok and New York, the thousands of aid workers on the border still succeeded in getting the suffering that we witnessed daily into the world's conscience, and the world was not complacent. If the sympathy and compassion that landed in our warehouses was sometimes poorly selected, the welcome that families in America and Europe extended to Cambodian refugees who managed to reach a new homeland were not. At its height, the border relief absorbed the physical stamina and emotional strength of some five-thousand international and local aid workers from all different backgrounds and working cultures. Our forged apparatus, our common mission, our shared humanitarian objective is what, in the end, survived political intransigence and the demoralization that comes from accusations of complicity. It is what allowed us to save lives that had very nearly already been lost when they lay themselves down at the border.

SWEDEN

Malmö

CYPRUS

TANZANIA

PART 2

THE MAKING OF A FIELD OFFICER

CHAPTER 8
True Grit

I N MY PROFESSIONAL CAREER as an employee of the United Nations, I have served six Secretaries General; joined four UN agencies; been posted to seventeen duty stations; operated in nine emergencies and travelled to close to a hundred countries. I have been shot at, taken hostage, bombed, threatened and evacuated. I've witnessed the evidence of massacres and famines. I've put colleagues in body bags.

My experience is neither extraordinary nor strictly average. Over the years I have met colleagues whose global scope is greater, whose breadth of experience is broader, and whose brushes with disaster are more numerous. I have also crossed paths with plenty of career servicemen who have avoided "field-work" yet achieved important humanitarian objectives from the relative safety of New York, Geneva or Vienna.

I do not pretend that my story is unique or, conversely, stere typical of an international civil servant or humanitarian emergency aid worker. Aid workers, like all beings, come in many sorts: There are the "crisis cowboys" who, like the foreign correspondents whose datelines are a chronicle of wars and natural disasters, show up regularly at every emergency, no matter how loud or how silent. There are the global citizens who make every continent their home and absorb the local culture everywhere they land. And there are the technical wizards whose skill is to apply proven systems universally, with little regard for cultural, social or political specificities.

I am a little bit of all those types. I assess an emergency without romance and with a tested blueprint in hand. I put my shoulder to the wheel and roll up my sleeves. I challenge authority and respect *realpolitik*. And when I look back on an operation, I remember the huge sense of accomplishment that was the big picture, as well as the small pleasures like a home-cooked meal that made it possible to focus on the big picture after a long day. I consider a nice pasta and a glass of Chianti critical resources for the health of a tough, protracted operation.

"What is the most important trait to have if you want to work for the United Nations?" my students at the University of Lund, where I teach a master's course in international development sometimes ask. When they do, I begin to discourse on the key tenets of leadership, the importance of teamwork, the critical balance between high-level international crisis negotiation and "bush diplomacy", and the ability to focus on a shared objective rather than on the disputed path to getting there. I wander into personal anecdotes that sometimes contradict the tenets I am trying to teach: the fundamental goodness of the United Nations as a global institution and the basic value of an international, cooperative approach to development. But when I back up and look more closely at my own experience and at the qualities of those colleagues that have most inspired and informed me, I tell my students that if you want to work as a humanitarian for the United Nations and get a sense of true satisfaction from that work, you have to be prepared to never give up and to never quit.

"The most important trait …" I tell these eager young men and women with their sharp minds and their fingers poised over their laptops, "is grit."

Some of them even write it down.

CHAPTER 9

A Swedish Viking in Rio

I WAS BORN IN SWEDEN IN 1945. More specifically, I was born in the village of Bjarred in the Province of Skane, on October 23, 1945. My father saw great significance in that date – the eve of the founding of an institution intent on preventing another World War, a horror that he experienced on the front lines for four years. In my father's mind, the United Nations loomed large on the canvas of world progress, and he gave a starring role in that happy outlook to two Swedish statesmen whose moral authority, political experience and dedicated diplomacy were integral to the early UN: Raoul Wallenberg and Dag Hammarskjöld were my father's heroes and would become, in time, mine.

I grew up on a working farm that had been in my mother's family for centuries. My father, roped into agriculture by my bewitching mother, was a reluctant farmer, and though I adored the hustle and bustle of the sudden influx of migrant workers who turned our home into a two-week long circus at harvest-time, I never gave much thought to making farming my future either. My fascination lay twenty-five kilometers south of our sleepy fishing village ... in Malmö.

The largest port on the Oresund Sound, linking the Baltic and North Seas, Malmö was Scandinavia's busiest harbor. The cargo ships that docked there unloaded the world on its docks: Coffee from Brazil and Yemen, bananas and pineapples from Trinidad and Jamaica spices from Zanzibar and India and putrid hides from Argentina and Uruguay.

Just beyond the docks were the most trafficked waters in the world, second only to the Panama Canal. This was the world that called to me. It called to all the boys in Bjarred, a backwater that lacked even a movie house. We were of Viking descent, after all. Why wouldn't we dream of the open seas?

By the time I was a teenager, I was riding my bicycle to Malmö daily during the school holidays, not just to goggle at the massive boats and dream of their exotic ports of call, but to earn my own money and a place among the scurrying dockworkers. I was employed as a messenger for one of the shipping companies, a cycling gopher. I was good at my job and very reliable. It didn't take me long to graduate from "hey, you!" - the bike messenger, to "hey, Kricke!" - the most trusted go-between for the customs officers, dockers, ship crews, hookers and drunks of Malmö port.

My favorite assignments were deliveries to the docked ships. There was nothing more magical than marching up the gangway to the bridge, where I would hand over my papers to the first mate. If the captain offered me a soft drink, I would spend another ten minutes in heaven, fancying myself dressed in sailor's whites as I piloted the ship through heavy storms.

This was an era when commercial ports were not yet mechanized. Unloading the hold of a single cargo ship without cranes or containers required the non-stop work of a sizable crew; and Malmö docked four or five ships a day. Like the workers who showed up at my family's farm at harvest time, the men who swarmed the shipping offices every day at sunrise were transient men who worked for lunch. Many of them were equally interested in that night's pint. Malmö's docks were full of strong men with bulging muscles and wind-blown faces. They were also full of scrappy characters with stringy forearms and sharp red noses. Between the two, truth be told, I rather preferred the fighters and drunks. Perhaps because they were the ones who had the time and inclination to entertain me with their stories. I learned a great deal from my fellow dockworkers— how to filter moonshine and how to smuggle ladies onto the ships at sundown. In return, I looked out for them. Many a pre-dawn morning found me corralling wayward dockers to the ships in various states of sobriety.

But my real idol-worship was directed towards the seaman. Because it wasn't enough, this whiff of the world that blew through windows of the shipping office (on a good day, smelling of the spice isles and on a bad day, of rotten rawhide). It wasn't enough to stand on the bridge daydreaming. I wanted to leave the harbor and see the world.

This was easier said than done at the age of sixteen, and I had to use quasi-legal means and all my port connections to secure a passport and the required documents to work on a ship. This was fairly simple with the connections I had made at the port. I enlisted my brother in my getaway plans, and on a cool spring dawn I boarded the *M/S Argentina* en route to Rio de Janeiro. Filial guilt seized me just before we weighed anchor, and I called my parents, who, tight-lipped and displaying admirable restraint, requested that I please keep in touch.

Though it would probably look like a life-boat next to today's enormous cargo ships, which run up to 400 meters in length, the *Argentina*, with her 8,000 ton hold, was the largest ship I had every seen. Breathless with excitement, I approached the steward and asked for my dress whites. He dashed my hopes by directing me to the kitchens at the bottom of the ship. My uniform, I learned, would be a dirty apron. I was starting my seafaring life as a dishwasher.

The mess, rank and dank as a dungeon, had no view, of course, of the sea. As I grappled with greasy plates that refused to come clean under cold water, I struggled to contain my disappointment and resentment. I worked from 5am until 10pm, cleaning up after four shifts of sailors. My day was not done until I had helped the cook, a sea-weary grouch, douse the floors and stoves with boiling water to kill off the roaches. Within a week I had only one objective: to get the hell off the *Argentina*.

In fact it would be a full year before I returned to Sweden. This adventure-filled year taught me many lessons – including the truth that not all adventures are glorious or even enjoyable. Viking blood be damned. My year at sea was enough to cure me of my romantic nautical dreams.

We had only just left Swedish waters when we ran into rough weather. A hurricane in the Bay of Biscaya washed our deck cargo – a fleet of Volvo trucks – into the sea and nearly capsized the vessel. Luckily there were no human casualties to join the automotive cargo at the bottom of the ocean, and we limped our way into the Canary Islands, where we spent a few days waiting for repairs.

The journey across the Atlantic lasted a little over two weeks. In my limited free time, I kept an eye out for dolphins and whales and palled around with the three other adolescents on board. My bunkmate, a native of Stockholm named Robert, was my closest friend amid an unfriendly crowd. Like me, he was from a middle-class family. He, too, had signed up with stars in his eyes, and the disparity between his imagined adventure and the reality of our shipboard experience was tougher, I think, on him than on me. Thrown into the rough company of seasoned sailors who had little regard for our mental and physical health, Robert and I supported each other the best we could. In fact, I probably owe this kid my life. One day I found myself locked in the walk-in freezer. It was Robert who eventually came looking for me. When he opened the door and found me huddled the shivering resignation that I would die at sea in a meat freezer, Robert looked like an angel.

We docked in Rio de Janeiro just in time to celebrate the last of Carnival, the weeklong bacchanalia that marks the end of Lent for Catholics and a good pretext to masquerade, dance, drink and generally revel for everyone else. I wasn't averse. On our scant per diem, we took shore leave and danced for three days and nights. Hung over and happy, Robert and I reported back to the ship and continued south along the coast, picking up cargos of bananas in the small harbors along the way to Buenos Aires. There we unloaded the Volvos that had survived the storm and refilled the empty hold with stinking wet animal hides.

We had just finished the loading when the city was rocked with violence – civil unrest was back on the agenda in coup-addled Argentina, and the supporters of exiled President Juan Peron were waging a street war. Anticipating escalation, the captain ordered an expedited departure. I was both disappointed and relieved to leave the city, which was counting the dead and preparing for more.

Meanwhile, a bigger crisis was brewing in the Caribbean waters to our north -- a crisis that brought the entire world to a frightened standstill for two weeks as Washington and Moscow came within a trigger finger of nuclear war.

The October 1962 standoff over Soviet missiles in Cuba would become one of the most important events of the 20th century – a symbol of the human race's vulnerability to nuclear annihilation. For a boy far from home, it was a lesson in appreciation. Faced with the possibility that I would never see my family again, I became deeply homesick.

On October 22, American President John F. Kennedy announced that he was prepared to retaliate against an installation of Soviet missiles in Cuba. He ordered the US armed forces on full readiness, DEFCON 3, and a naval blockade of 180 ships around Cuban waters. Foreign ships throughout Latin America were ordered to stay in port until the crisis was resolved. The crew of the *M/S Argentina* was confined indefinitely to the harbor of Rio de Janeiro, about 6,500 kilometers south of Havana.

My anxiety grew the next day when Robert, who had gone into the city to escape the tension on board, failed to return. Tragically, he was soon found very nearby – slumped behind a warehouse with a bullet in his head. Nuclear war, perpetual exile, and never seeing my family again, worse-case scenarios no less enormous than the unsolved murder of my young friend, vanished from my thoughts. But when those thoughts returned, Robert's death had been absorbed into them and intensified my fear. Now I was truly alone.

Days later, Russian guns on Cuban soil shot down a US spy plane. Irate and cognizant of the potential ramifications, President Kennedy requested the diplomatic intervention of the United Nations. UN Secretary General, U Thant, asked the Soviets to deescalate. But the debates in the Security Council, which we listened to through the ship's loudspeakers compliments of Voice of America, revealed little progress. Indeed, the situation grew more critical by the hour, intensified by the fact that in crucial moments, communication broke down altogether.

At some point, we would learn much later, the crew of the nuclear-armed Soviet submarine deep in the waters off Cuba fell under the notion that war had in fact broken out between the US and the Soviet Union. Unable to make contact with Moscow from their depth, the three officers on board had to come to a decision. Two of the officers wanted to launch their nuclear payload. Lieutenant Vasily Arkhipov, second-in-command, convinced them to stand down and await orders from the Kremlin.

On October 25, United States Secretary of State Adlai Stevenson directly confronted the Soviet Ambassador to the UN in the Security Council chambers saying, *"Sir, let me ask you one simple question: Do you, Ambassador Zorin, deny that the U.S.S.R. has placed and is placing medium- and intermediate-range missiles and sites in Cuba? Yes or no—don't wait for the translation—yes or no?"*

We listened to the crackle of silence over the radio waves, followed by Stevenson's indignation: *"You can answer yes or no. You have denied they exist. I want to know if I understood you correctly. I am prepared to wait for my answer until hell freezes over, if that's your decision. And I am also prepared to present the evidence in this room."*

And then, as we listened, mesmerized by the showdown, Adlai Stevenson set up a white board and showed the Soviet Ambassador Valerian Zorin and the members of the Security Council photographs taken by US spy planes over San Christobel, Cuba. Helpfully for those of us on board the *Argentina*, Stevenson explained what we couldn't see over the radio: *"These photographs clearly show six of these missiles on trailers and three erectors."*

I often think of that moment – the moment I understood the significance not just of Mr. Stevenson's smoking gun, but also of his decision to brandish it where he did: in the Security Council of the United Nations. I had been raised, like many Swedes, with a profound respect for the UN. Not only was the organization a response to the "scourge of war" that Sweden, despite its political neutrality, had observed from a front-row seat, but it was a global institution led for most of its first decade by a Swede, Dag Hammarskjöld.

I used to think that the simple fact that we have not had a world war since the UN charter was signed was evidence of its worth. I believed that if the great powers are given a forum to wage war in words, then the likelihood of a land war is automatically reduced. The Cuban Missile Crisis was a perfect example of peaceable, internationally observed, conflict resolution.

That is how it impressed me at the time, and that is how it impresses me to this day, which is why it pains me to concede that in the 21st century, the chambers of the United Nations have repeatedly been used as forums for warmongers. Colin Powell may have thought that he was stepping into

Adlai Stevenson's large shoes when he presented the Security Council with his own photographic evidence of weapons of mass destruction in Iraq in February 2003. What we did not know, and what the unwitting war veteran himself did not know, was that the evidence was "dead wrong." True, the Security Council did not endorse the US invasion of Iraq. But it also failed to prevent it.

A quarter of a century has passed since we resolved geopolitical crises through the lens of a bipolar world. The Cuban Crisis may have seemed at the time an exceedingly close brush with nuclear annihilation, but the very fact that it was mutually assured destruction is what allowed to UN to broker a peaceful resolution. In the post-Cold War world, hostilities tend to be asymmetric. Potential losses may well be enormous, but generally one-sided. The United Nations, it must be remembered, is not endowed with its own independent power. The highest decision-making body within the organization is the Security Council, and most squarely with the Permanent Members – namely the US, Russia, France, Britain and China, aka the Allied victors and big powers of 1945. To borrow historian Maggie Black's explanation: the power within the UN structure "will always reside where power resides in the world." While it is debatable whether power in the 21st century really resides as assuredly in those Permanent Member states as it did in 1945, there is no question that it does not reside with the Tutsis of Rwanda, the Bosnians of Sarajevo or the civilians of Syria. When these populations are threatened with destruction, it is a one-way threat. And when these hostilities are not successfully defused and end in grave human losses, it is the shame not of the United Nations but of the world powers the UN structure mirrors.

Two days after Adlai Stevenson's dramatic presentation in the Security Council negotiators from both sides met in a Chinese restaurant where, legend has it, they hammered out a deal to avert nuclear war. So in addition to Soviet submarine lieutenant Vasily Arkhipov and the Russian Ambassador to the United Nations, Valerian Zorin, we have Peking duck to thank for averting World War III.

One month later I was home. My parents met me at the dock, and I threw myself at them in grateful emotion. To my parents' infinite credit, they neither lectured me for my waywardness nor pressed me for details about my year at sea. Instead, they waited for me to broach the subject and to admit that my expectations had been naïve. I did eventually concede that, in retrospect, I had not been prepared for the adventure.

But that was then, and this is now. Today I look back at 1962 as my first test. And I passed. I didn't quit. I didn't jump overboard. I cried more than once, but I never gave up. And in November 1962, I was the happiest boy who ever debarked in Malmö harbor.

CHAPTER 10
Training for War and Peace

AFTER THE CUBAN MISSILE CRISIS, the Cold War cooled, but just slightly. The ideological differences between the Soviet Union and the United States were by now a part of the geographic landscape. No matter how apolitical its population, every European nation lived in acute awareness of an Iron Curtain dividing former allies and neighbors. In Sweden, where the government had found a middle way between the imperfect models of capitalism and communism, there was palpable awareness of the voracious appetite of the Russian bear next door to us. Beginning in 1956 with the invasion of Hungary, our massive superpower neighbor made clear its intention to turn allies into satellites and buffer states into political subjects.

The main impact of the Cold War on Sweden was a heavy investment in a combat-ready army of national defense. Military service was obligatory, and I completed basic training at age eighteen. I had finished my secondary education and I determined that if I had to serve, I would do so in the most challenging environment possible. My father, who had served through the entire four years of World War II, tried mightily to dissuade me, but I applied and was accepted for the *Kustjagarskolan,* the training programme for the Swedish Royal Marines.

In the fall of 1964, after an overnight train journey on a third class bench, I stumbled onto the platform at the Vaxholm marine base with my fellow recruits to the sound of barking disgust from our new sergeant: "Who the hell is responsible for selecting this miserable bunch!"

The Royal Marines, the equivalent to Britain's elite forces or to the US Navy Seals, had no room for mediocrity. With an emphasis on extreme physical endurance and mental tenacity, the yearlong training programme demanded far more stamina than I had mustered to combat anxiety on deck of the *Argentina* or fatigue in her rancid kitchen. But I was determined to succeed at any cost.

Only a quarter of the young men in training would graduate from the *Kustjagarskolan*. I was among them. I had marched through blizzards without food and water. I had been dropped with my skis into the northernmost reaches of Sweden's desolate arctic territory and navigated solo with only a compass back to our base. We trained in teams as well as solo: paddling 275 kilometers in open water for three days and nights; surviving simulated week-long hostilities without supplies; enduring mental resilience tests that pitted us against all sorts of hardships including, at the end of a particularly famished week, the gift of raw meat with no implement to cook it.

These were absolutely pivotal years in my personal growth and professional future. What I learned (beyond how to orient myself by the stars and how to wring a chicken's neck) was this: Survival depends on team cohesion; and team cohesion depends on strong leadership.

I graduated from the *Kustjagarskolan* with merit and a handsome uniform but without a penny in my pocket. So when some of my fellow marines told me to consider a stint as a UN peacekeeper, a temporary but well-paid assignment that would feel like a cakewalk after our rigorous training, I did.

One year later I was seated in a non-descript classroom at an army base in central Sweden learning an entirely different skill set from that which I had been taught in the frostbitten northern reaches. Unlike the torturous drilling I underwent to become a marine, the training to become an international peacekeeper was short and simple: Keep calm, control crowds, and do not use force. That was it. The armed forces of the United Nations, we learned, may be an army, but it is an *invited* army. As such, our sword and our shield were no more than the logo on our helmets and flags – the UN globe nestled in the olive branches of peace.

It was Dag Hammarskjöld who created the UN peacekeeping programme. Hammarskjöld was Sweden's darling, along with other proud sons, Raul Wallenberg and Folke Bernadotte. Wallenberg and Bernadotte were Swedish diplomats whose shared legacy was the salvation of tens of thousands of people from the Nazi Holocaust. Both were shabbily rewarded for their efforts. Wallenberg, who issued protective passports for as many as 15,000 Hungarian Jews in Nazi-occupied Budapest, disappeared into the Soviet Gulag upon the city's liberation by the Red Army. Bernadotte, who negotiated the release of 30,000 prisoners from German concentration camps during the war, was dispatched with less discretely. In 1948 he was assassinated by extremists in Jerusalem who resented his role as a UN peacemaker intent on preventing precisely the discord that continues to roil the Holy Land today. Both men are revered in Sweden to this day. But it was UN Chief Hammarskjöld who was my father's hero.

As only the second man to hold the position of Secretary General of the United Nations, Hammarskjöld had a considerable role in defining the post before his untimely and (much speculated-upon) death in an airplane crash in 1961. He leaned more towards the General than the Secretary, and none of his successors have had that distinction: U Thant, the second SG (1961 – 1971) was not averse to keeping his key role in defusing the Cuban Missile Crisis under the public radar; Kurt Waldheim (1972-1981) was diminished by a late-breaking association with the Nazi party, a revelation that, amazingly, did not seriously damage the integrity of the UN but certainly did not help it; Javier Perez de Cuelar (1982-1991), an elegant man, was more diplomatic than dogged; Boutros Boutros Ghali (1992-1996) endeavored to carve out more turf for the independent body and was denied a second term. As a result, he remains the UN's only single term Secretary; Kofi Annan (1997-2006) was perhaps the strongest leader of the UN since Hammarskjöld because, as an SG who came through the rank-and-file, he held the respect and allegiance of the entire organization; Ban Ki-Moon, the present chief, was a surprise selection and as a quiet functionary devoid of much charisma, a stark contrast to his predecessors.

Halfway through his second term, the Korean has surpassed initial expectations and proved to be a forceful voice for the organization, particularly on issues of climate change, women's empowerment and human rights.

Hammarskjöld's near universal approval was not due just to his leadership qualities and character; it was also a product of its time. The men who followed him have been beholden to more stakeholders and burdened with far more conflicts to defuse. They also had to contend with the fallout of failure. Once the novelty of a supra-national experiment in global cooperation passed, the United Nations quite naturally became a potential nuisance for self-interested members like the United States whose Secretary of State chided U Thant for daring to criticize US policy in Vietnam: "Who do you think you are? A country?"

The Secretary General has tremendous moral influence but extremely limited usable power. This weakness comes down to the lack of a political mandate for the UN. As the head of the UN, the Secretary General serves at the whim of the body's most powerful members while he tries to persuade them to join a consensus that may not preserve their national interest. There are checks and balances in the system, it is true. The Secretary General, it should be noted, is never selected from a nation with a permanent seat in the Security Council. And just as I have argued for the symbolic force of a UN presence in conflict zones, I would argue that the Secretary General has a significant power as a figurehead and a man with a tremendous bully pulpit. I only rue the fact that the world has turned a deaf ear to the moral underpinnings of his message. Ban Ki-Moon has delivered strong words against the forces of brutality at work today and, significantly, on the importance of tackling global warning. He is not alone as a voice ignored.

I always tell my students that the job of the Secretary General is the most challenging job in the world, but that does not mean it is not one to aspire to. It is always a good practice to set the bar high. And the bar does not get much higher, in my opinion, than the Dag Hammarskjöld model. His judgment was never impaired by neutrality, and his neutrality was never compromised by his own belief in liberty. His handling of the Suez crisis, the first test of the UN's ability to stave off hostilities between Big Power armies, is a case in point.

In 1956, Britain and France invaded Egypt to protect their interests in the Suez Canal. Hammarskjöld responded boldly, asserting the UN's authority and responsibility to international security. By hitting upon a neutral, independent army of observers to replace British and French troops, Hammarskjöld allowed the former imperial powers an honorable withdrawal from the region. The United Nations Emergency Force in Sinai (UNEF), a command of 6,000 soldiers provided by eleven countries, was the first-ever international peacekeeping deployment. It had been in position for nearly a decade, tamping down tensions between Egypt and Israel, when in May 1967, the Egyptian government ordered all UN soldiers out of the Sinai, effective immediately.

By then, I was one month into my own deployment as a UN peacekeeper. I was one month away from experiencing first hand how complicated the role of peacekeeper can be when there is no peace to keep.

CHAPTER 11

Artemis Road

Cyprus, a rhino-head-shaped island in the eastern Mediterranean, is not called "Aphrodite's Island" for nothing. Spectacularly beautiful and cursed with jealous rivalries, it has been fought over for by fractious Phoenicians, Romans, Byzantines and Ottomans. The island gained independence from the British Empire in 1960 and immediately descended into internecine warring between its native Greek and Turkish populations. Hostilities continued unabated until 1964 when the Cypriot government called upon the UN to send a peacekeeping force.

When I arrived in Cyprus in the spring of 1967, there were several thousand so-called "blue helmets" deployed throughout the country. As a group officer, I was no different from the other young recruits. But an unusual double retirement in my group promoted me quickly up the ranks until, at just twenty-two years of age, I found myself the youngest platoon commander in the history of Swedish peacekeeping.

The thirty men that I commanded joined a larger battalion of Swedish soldiers stationed at Camp Goldfish, a base outside Famagusta. A beautiful harbor town on the eastern coast of the island, Famagusta was inhabited predominantly by Greek Cypriots and was, outwardly, quiet and conflict-free. For several weeks we enjoyed the natural beauty and excellent cuisine of our hosts. We saw the divided country on purely culinary terms: On the Greek side was the slow cooked lamb shanks served with tomato and cucumber salad, fresh bread and ice cold Keo beer. When we ventured into the Turkish enclave in the Old Town, we were treated to *dolma*s, grilled octopus, and the cloudy, anise liqueur that the Turks call *raki* and the Greeks call *ouzo*. As the island's main cargo port, Famagusta felt like home to me when strolling down to the docks, breathing in the aromas of the world converging.

Initially it was easy to keep peace in the quiet of Famagusta, where for some time the only action we saw was the explosion of a camp latrine. This incendiary event, the result of too much kerosene poured into the privy by the unfortunate underling tasked with latrine-cleaning duties, was a debacle not just in camp, where our entire company was exposed to flying fecal material, but more broadly in town, where both Turks and Greeks who heard the explosion quickly mobilized for war. "Stinky," as the bungling latrine-cleaner was uncharitably nicknamed, was strongly reprimanded for nearly setting off an international incident, and we fell back into relative quiet and even boredom.

But some weeks later, another instance of mistaken firefight, this one 100 kilometers south of Camp Goldfish in the Greek-held city of Limassol, did indeed escalate, and it was my platoon that was dispatched to get it under control.

The call came in around noon from the peacekeeping unit's headquarters in Nicosia. An old man – an ethnic Greek who, like all his countrymen, relished the taste of the small birds that filled the Cyprus skies – had begun his morning by hunting for lunch. Hoping to bag a few swallows, he instead alarmed a Turkish neighbor across Artemis Road, the informal border between the hostile and heavily armed communities. Assuming the shots aimed at birds were in fact the shots of a sniper, the Turkish man picked up his own gun and returned fire, wounding his neighbor. All that had been in the morning. Now, several hours later, they were still shooting. And there were casualties.

As reporting duty officer, I took the call and mobilized my platoon. Within the hour we were trundling south in a convoy of armed personnel carriers, one of which I was driving myself. We arrived to find ourselves in the middle of, not a minor skirmish, but a full-blown firefight – one that the appearance of our armed vehicles and blue flags failed to quell. I exited the APC and attempted to verbally engage the snipers on either side of the road. I found myself not merely ignored – but targeted. This was, to put it mildly, an unexpected turn of events. We had been made to believe that a simple show of force – a convoy of UN vehicles raising a cloud of dust that mere bullet kicks could not compete with – would send the hotheads back to their gardens. But they showed no interest in hanging up their guns. The smiles and waves that we had received in the markets of Famagusta were memories. We were under fire.

I followed protocol. I radioed back to Famagusta, where my commander, in turn, radioed headquarters in Nicosia. Nicosia then followed the chain of command up to the Department of Peacekeeping Operations headquarters (DPKO) in New York. I was instructed to stand by for orders. As foreign soldiers located on sovereign territory by invitation only, we could not intervene in the skirmish. As UN peacekeepers with a mandate to de-escalate the conflict, we could not leave the scene and allow the fighting to spill across the road. We were in a dangerous limbo and in the crosshairs, as well.

I hunkered down in the shade of my APC and pondered this. All of my training in leadership was at odds with my more recent indoctrination in peacekeeping. On Artemis Road, I was not a commanding officer in the Swedish marines, nor was I an employee of the United Nations. I was just a body on loan to the UN to provide a buffer. My men and I were under fire, but I was forbidden from defending them, since my job was to quell hostilities, not to join them.

The next time I radioed my commander, it was to tell him that we were completely besieged, our exit blocked by more militants with significant firepower. Again, the orders were to hold fast and not to engage. Hours passed and then days. In today's operations, the relay from flash point to headquarters would take 20 minutes. In 1967, we were still using WWII-era communications. It took three days for reinforcements to arrive. By the time they did, my men and I had dug trenches alongside our vehicles to shield ourselves from the artillery. We had utterly failed to subdue the fighting. In fact, the isolated case of mistaken gunfire had sparked itchy trigger fingers throughout the country. The UN peacekeeping force was kept busy for months reestablishing a calm status quo that held until 1974 when a coup by Turkish Cypriots further entrenched the ethnic divisions of the small island nation.

More than three decades later, there is still ethnic division in Cyprus, and there is still a UN peacekeeping presence. Famagusta is effectively a ghost town, its population having been forcibly relocated by the occupying Turkish army. When I tell my students this, they are quick to interpret the UN peacekeeping presence on Cyprus as a failure. I am equally quick to correct them. The purpose of the blue helmets is to prevent bloodshed and war crimes. It is not to enforce fraternal harmony. If the Greeks and the Turks still cannot find it in their hearts to live peacefully side-by-side, that is their problem. If the presence of a UN buffer zone is still protecting a decades-long cease-fire along Artemis Road, that is to its credit.

I WAS, AND STILL AM, VERY PROUD of being an officer of the United Nations peacekeeping force. Without this experience, I would not have been as successful later in my career in moments when fostering a calm, non-antagonistic understanding among differing factions was imperative to execute lifesaving operations and logistics. But my harrowing three-day experience on Artemis Road filled me with questions still relevant today: *Are the locals shooting at us or in spite of us? Is our presence welcome or only conditionally so?* And perhaps most urgently *Why the hell shouldn't I shoot back, if only to protect my men?*

I hardly needed to get lost in the fog of war to understand the answer to the last question: Had I used firepower to extract my fellow peacekeepers from Artemis Road, I would have almost certainly succeeded only in fanning the flames of what was a localized flare-up. But in the decades since my stint as a peacekeeper, thousands of other blue helmet officers have faced a worse dilemma – their allegiance to neutrality makes them powerless to defend innocent civilians against the violence of militants.

It is one of the most common criticisms leveled at the United Nations: *Why don't they stop the killing?* It was asked when pictures emerged of the mass graves of Srebrenica. It was asked when Rwandans were massacred with impunity and when Russian troops invaded South Ossetia even as UNOMIG, the UN observer force in the enclave, did just that – observe.

My answer is Artemis Road. The 1967 siege of thirty well-armed Swedish soldiers by a handful of Cypriot villagers bearing ancient rifles was the first indicator of the fundamental limitations of the UN Department of Peacekeeping. They are the same limitations that stymie all of the UN's most worthy activities —an inability to act without sanctioned approval, an inviolable adherence to bureaucratic process, and a dependence on cooperative agreement. My students sometimes pull their hair out over my Cyprus story, but I assure them that the weaknesses it showcases are, if not desirable, inevitable.

The reason is simple. The United Nations was founded as a collective body, and its legitimacy still rests on the approval and cooperation of its members. These were easy to secure in the years following a brutal World War, when the nations who agreed to be united numbered just fifty-one. Today there are nearly two hundred member states, and collective agreement is much more difficult to come by. Cyprus was the fourth peacekeeping mission authorized by the United Nations. Since then there have been sixty-eight operations – the vast majority initiated since 1988, which is to say since the end of the Cold War. Each mission has been subject to the same constraints that are inviolable in the peacekeeping mandate: consent of governed parties; impartiality; and exclusion of force.

The troops who march into troubled territories wearing the blue helmet (or, when in non-active duty, the blue beret) are not out to score victories or to settle territorial disputes. They are not dispatched to maintain a balance of power, only a balance of peace. Peace can only be done (both legally and practically) with the consent of the governing power of the nation in need of peace. Bashar Assad, for example, is no such governor, and Syria has no peace to maintain. I have never stepped foot in Syria and I, like the rest of the worl too easily forget, as the civil war enters its fifth year, that in 2012 there were UN observers stationed in Syria. But within months of their deployment, hostilities escalated to a level incompatible with peacekeeping mandate. The UN had no choice but to withdraw those forces at the end of their mandate in August 2012, and they have not returned since. The world asks "Why?"

The answer is simple and human: The five permanent members of the United Nations Security Council, all of whom have veto powers, have not reached an agreement on sanctions against the Syrian Government and are unable to negotiate with the opposing forces for any kind of a truce, even on humanitarian grounds. The impasse has created one of the most unstable regions in the world and one of the largest human exoduses in modern times. I certainly do not envy my colleague Stephan DeMistura. He is a long-serving and highly competent UN official who has been on the political humanitarian frontline his entire career. But as the Secretary General's Special Representative for Syria he has been given a formidable challenge that will test his skills.

There are presently sixteen peacekeeping forces mobilized around the world. A handful of them, like that in Cyprus, are keeping a very old peace. For example, the very first peacekeeping force ever deployed is still observing the disputed Golan Heights nearly sixty-five years after its inception. And what is the reason for the longevity of these operations? Deployments are generally in response to domestic conflicts, rather than disputed borders. In these situations, where the aggrieved party is in opposition to the state that speaks its mind in the UN General Assembly, the UN emblem often becomes a target rather than a shield. This has been the case in Haiti, Darfur, Lebanon, Afghanistan, East Timor, Somalia and Liberia. More than 3,000 peacekeepers have died in service since the formation of the DPKO. I was in close proximity to the murders of nearly thirty of them on a hot morning in Mogadishu in 1993. They were Pakistanis, men who were slaughtered while attempting to inspect a weapons depot in what was certainly the most dangerous city on the planet at that time. And though their loss shook the Pakistani government, that nation continues to provide a disproportionate contingent of its troops to international peacekeeping efforts.

It has taken many years of observation of the UN peacekeepers in some of the world's most challenging, violent conflicts for me to appreciate the number of lives they have saved and the sacrifices they make to do so. The fallen are unsung heroes who do not get the recognition they deserve. And still the mind boggles at the implicit challenge: an effectively unarmed army tasked with enforcing borders or agreements under dangerous conditions that even shiny-shoed diplomats in the halls of the General Assembly have trouble agreeing on.

To the UN's great credit, there is now recognition of the intolerable risk it puts its borrowed soldiers at when it deploys them to intractable and incredibly violent internal conflicts like those in Congo, CAR, Sudan or East Timor without the right to defend themselves. Peacekeepers are now empowered to use firearms to defend themselves and, even more significantly, to defend innocent civilians. Not long ago Secretary General Ban Ki-Moon denounced the attack on a UN compound in South Sudan where thousands of ethnic minorities sheltered as a war crime. Two dozen civilians were killed by the armed mob, but more would have died had the Ugandan peacekeepers stationed in the region not fired back.

Today there are 120,000 men and women employed in UN peacekeeping or observer missions around the world. They work under extremely difficult conditions, far from their families. They wear the blue helmets of neutrality, but their uniforms are those of their national armies. With sixteen operations open – the largest number of operations running simultaneously in the history of the UN – it is all the more important that peacekeeping missions be financially sustainable and cost-effective. The blue helmets look much different from my days in Cyprus, where the majority of the deployed peacekeepers were from western, wealthy nations. Today it is Pakistan, India, Bangladesh and Nigeria that provide the bulk of the DPKO manpower, while wealthy member states provide funding for the operations.

An interesting symbol of the maturity of the UN DPKO can be seen today in Sierra Leone. Fifteen years ago, the UN sent peacekeepers to monitor the highly fragile cease-fire that ended an appallingly bloody civil war. After an initial deployment of 6,000 troops proved insufficient, the force was tripled and helped end the war decisively in January 2002; but only after rebel fighters had taken five hundred peacekeepers hostage for two and a half months, almost prompting a pullout. But the mission prevailed. Today, fifteen years after the peacekeeping operation was authorized, the UN has recognized Sierra Leone's transformation.

Once a lawless state in need of outside peacekeepers, today the country contributes soldiers to peacekeeping efforts worldwide. The President of Sierra Leone, Ernest Bai Koroma, called the transformation, "healing therapy for a country that has emerged from a massively devastating internal conflict," noting that such therapy was a victory in a country that was once "a byword for humanitarian crisis."

ONCE I REMOVED THE BLUE HELMET on my return from Cyprus, I never considered a return to a soldier's life. But my career in emergency and humanitarian operations has brought me repeatedly into the realm of the military – whether that of a trained junta, irregular militias, or the valiant peacekeepers whose mandate is more hampered, but more admirable, than any other force on the planet. And I have somehow managed to "speak the language" of them all.

CHAPTER 12

First Taste of Africa

Just as the legacy of Dag Hammarskjöld was beginning to fade from the international scene, another Swede was rising to take his place as a strong-minded, outspoken and polarizing figure focused on social justice and foreign development. Olaf Palme, who would later become Prime Minister, was serving as the Swedish Minister of Education when I returned home from Cyprus in 1967.

Palme was a strident defender of Sweden's Cold War non-alignment and an outspoken critic of imperialism, particularly the American brand. As Prime Minister, he took a very prominent position against the US involvement in Vietnam . He shocked the world when when he stood by the side of Premiere Le Duc Tho during a demonstration in Stockholm.

Palme believed in the ideals of Africa's progressive movement and was influential in funneling Swedish foreign aid towards support of the continent's most radical socialist states. Some of this assistance was political. Much of it came in the form of technical development. Such was the *Fredskarem* programme, the Swedish Peace Corps. Modeled on US President John F. Kennedy's Peace Corps, *Fredskarem* was a young body of volunteer ambassadors bearing friendship, manpower and technical training to countries emerging from colonial systems into independence. But if Kennedy's idealism masked an ideological objective to align these new nations against the spread of communism and Soviet influence, Sweden's Peace Corps served at a counterbalance – at least in Dar es Salaam, where I arrived in the spring of 1969.

At that time, Tanzania was home to one of the newest socialist experiments in Africa. President Julius Nyerere had just outlined an ambitious vision for his five-year old republic. The Arusha Declaration emphasized civil freedom, economic justice, and a classless society. It launched the policy of *ujamaa*, or "brotherhood," a collectivization programme that, in theory, promised to transform society and to usher in economic development and social reform. In practice, it bankrupted the country.

My fellow volunteers and I had been given some basic training in Swahili and Tanzanian culture, but we knew next to nothing about Nyerere's collectivization programme. Nor did we know how much money Sweden was investing in *ujamaa* through soft contributions. Over time, we saw that our eager agreement to dig wells and build roads, health centers and schools for a pittance of a per diem was just one arm of Sweden's embrace of radical political agendas in Africa.

In fact, the University of Tanzania in Dar es Salaam was a socialist incubator assisted by Warsaw Bloc countries. Many of Africa's most radical young socialists began their indoctrination in a cell that met next to our *Fredskarem* offices in the suburbs. It was rumoured that Che Guevara was on its faculty. Whenever I went into the capital to report on the rural project I was assigned to, I did so down the road from where Yoweri Museveni, Samora Machel, Joseph Kabila, and Joachim Chisanu were planning the overthrow of oppressive regimes in Uganda and Mozambique and other newly formed African countries.

As volunteers committed to helping build *ujamaa*, we were dispatched to villages far from the capital where we would spend the next two years living in native conditions and helping oversee infrastructure projects funded by our government. I was sent to a place called Mloka to supervise a water and sanitation project, the highlight of which was the construction of a water tower.

Mloka today is a popular safari hub located just outside the gates of the Selous Game Reserve, one of the largest wildlife reserves in the world. Forty years ago, however, Mloka was a 100-hut village where white faces were a rarity. Like all remote Tanzanian villages, it lacked all modern amenities including electricity, running water and basic medical services. Dar es Salaam was 300 kilometers away, and the closest radio was almost as far.

I had seen enough of the world by this time to know that I should expect a primitive life in the bush. But I had not yet been exposed to anything so completely different from my white, Euro-centric ideas of family, social behavior and lifestyle. Even my knowledge of poverty and class, formed by Scandinavian dockworkers and Latin American beggar children, were not applicable in this new environment. I was completely unprepared for Mloka, where putting food in the belly and keeping rain out of the huts were the primary daily objectives. Accustomed to sweating out hardship and boredom in the company of others – be it my platoon, messmates or fellow students – I was hit hard by the solitude of being the only *mzungu* in such a small, tight-knit community. Life among gibbon monkeys, wild cats and herds of elephants sharing the riverside was never boring, but there was still a sense of human isolation.

Initially, I was regarded in the village with suspicion and left to figure out the obvious on my own. The obvious being, firstly, that sleeping in a tent among anthills is a bad idea. I quickly moved into a vacant mud hut like those of the rest of the villagers. It did not take long, however, for me to win some credibility. I am forever in debt to my father for instilling me with knowledge of hunting and farming – skills that the village of Mloka recognized and admired. I made small talk with the men who owned goats and an occasional cow, and then once I acquired a game rifle and a hunter's license, I was not simply accepted, I was respected.

I hunted in the savannah surrounding the village, bringing back fresh antelope and wildebeest for my hosts. For a community accustomed to eating *ugali* porridge all day, every day, my contributions were a welcome feast. I took real satisfaction in the much-needed nutritional supplement I was bringing to my neighbors' limited diet. Aside from manioc root, corn and millet, there was very little in the village pantry. I always brought back sugar, rice and salt when I made supply trips to Dar es Salaam. These were considered luxuries in Mloka, where malnutrition was a leading cause of child death. I myself had attended more than one funeral for babies who had never managed to walk or for toddlers who lacked the strength.

My hunting side-job introduced me to the Selous Game Reserve Wardens, who patrolled the immense reserve on the lookout for poachers and wounded or aged animals. In time, the Wardens came to trust me and they invited me along on their patrols. My gun was better than any weapon in their arsenal, so they were grateful for my participation when it came time to putting down a wounded elephant or some other risky endeavor. Hiking the reserve for days at a time, wearing shorts and flip-flops and carrying nothing but their weapons and ammunition, the Selous wardens gave me insight that few of my fellow volunteers were afforded. As expert trackers from the Rufiji tribe, they were deeply knowledgeable about the land and totally devoted to their jobs. As impoverished men with families to feed, they were always torn by the temptation to become poachers themselves. My days and nights on patrol helped me gain fluency in the language and also in the land. We didn't discuss much more than animals, the weather, and the geographic terrain over those campfires in the black night, but it felt to me like the deepest philosophy.

During my days off, I also had the great honor of hunting with the Maasai, the semi-nomadic herders of the northern plains. The Maasai are pastoralists who measure their wealth in cattle, and they do not own guns, which are forbidden in their culture. They hunt with bow and arrow, and young men must kill a lion with a spear to be initiated into the warrior Goran class.

Though I never rose to that level of acceptance, I was invited to drink the symbolically spiritual (and god-awful) traditional drink made from fresh cow urine and cow blood. Getting that concoction down the gullet took every bit as much bravery as stalking a lion with a spear. I was also able to present the village chief with one of the largest impala he had ever seen, and in time I was accepted by this insular people into their *boma,* or living quarters.

I lived with them for just a few weeks, but their proud culture and their physical beauty impressed me deeply. It is a real sadness to me that modern boundaries and state regulation now infringe upon their nomadic lifestyle and threaten the simplicity of their culture. In more recent trips to Tanzania, I have seen these noble Maasai reduced to selling trinkets for tourists on the side of the road.

Of course, officially I had come to Tanzania not to track big cats and put down the occasional mad elephant, but to oversee the installation of a beautiful, bright water tower in the village of Mloka. This task was part of a country-wide water and sanitation project financed by the Government of Sweden. My job was to handle the finances and logistics at Mloka and other sites. I paid the vendors and construction workers and kept the project on course, so as to not get caught mid-construction by the rainy season when the village was cut off from the highway.

Such a position demanded, first of all, that I learn the patience of the bush and respect for its clock. Many an afternoon en route to or from the village, I would be at the mercy of the ferryman who could carry my car and me across the flooded Rufiji River. From one day to the next, the crossing-point would change and I would spend hours driving up and down river searching for the ferryman. I never broke my habit of asking others waiting or searching if they knew when he would arrive, despite the fact that the answer was always some version of that well-known local response to any temporal question: *"anytime from now..."* There was another common saying that helped me accept the futility of frustration in this culture. I would hear it frequently when I had arrived somewhere in the expectation of a meeting, a delivery or an answer. It was the message that: *"The man with the key has gone."* Sometimes there was no man. And sometimes there was no key. But if the man with the key had gone, there was no point in discussing it further.

Providing a poor, rural village with a clean, modern water supply was seen, I thought universally, as an excellent idea. I had no responsibility for the design or engineering of our water projects, but as the on-site supervisor, I hosted several international delegations interested in its progress. Though the blueprints and vendors were presented to me as a fait accompli, I did have some room to innovate local solutions. As the project progressed, I became increasingly aware of a disconnect between the international observers' starry-eyed visions and the indifference of the intended beneficiaries. As such, I looked for opportunities to engage the community more in the project. I was particularly proud of my initiative to produce gravel for the facility locally, rather than truck it in from across the country. In this way, I created jobs for hundreds of men and a sub-industry of lunch shacks and grocery stores sprung up around the gravel works. These were peasants from an arid land who were, for the first time, receiving payment in their hands. I believed I was making a difference in the small community, and I looked forward to the day when no woman, young or old, would have to walk to the river for her family's daily supply of water.

What the project organizers had failed to anticipate was that the people of Mloka liked their trek to the river. They worshipped the river, just as they revered all the forces of nature. Water from the river, in their eyes, was a gift from god. Water from a massive concrete tower built by outsiders was a suspicious intrusion. They wanted nothing to do with it.

No one had warned me that I might need to use my powers of persuasion in making the project a success. I was in charge of the books and logistics. Though I was well aware of the health benefits of clean water, it was not impressed upon me that such knowledge, if imparted to the villagers, might sway them towards using the improved infrastructure. Instead, I was kept busy ordering and transporting the steel and concrete that would result in the wondrous water tower, along with myriad other small parts that, had I taken the time to think about it, I would have recognized as another Achilles heel for the project. Mechanical infrastructure after all, requires maintenance. The system we were building was not sustainable for the simple reason that there was not a hardware store in two days travel time from Mloka.

I mention these oversights not to dwell on the failure of the Swedish government's contribution to Tanzania, but to point out two key components of a successful development project: sensitization and sustainability, neither of which were present in Mloka in 1979. No outside intervention, no matter how well intentioned, will be received as such if the donor fails to educate the beneficiaries of the value of the project and to provide them the means to sustain it. I know this not simply with the wisdom of time, but with the experience of working for UNICEF, an agency that puts sustainability and sensitization front and center in its programming.

Over the course of my first year in Mloka, I developed my own reservations about the ultimate worth of this costly infrastructural development. The gap between outside intention and the village's reception described, in a microcosm, the failings of Nyerere's *ujamaa*, which like all utopian impositions did not have the support of the people it hoped to transform.

But I must confess that, though I was outwardly eager to contribute to the village, I was thinking just as much about the personal dividends of such an opportunity. I had already determined that I wanted an international career and needed experience to grow one. I had no idea just how relevant my time in Tanzania would prove to be, and to this day I am aware of the implicit imbalance: For if I could have bestowed upon the people of Tanzania even half of the intangible gifts they gave me, I would have left it a much richer country indeed.

IN ADDITION TO TIME IN MLOKA and in the reserve, I was free to spend time in Dar es Salaam, where I always got a fresh dose of encouragement from the Peace Corps cadres who believed in our work. I shared an apartment in the capital with two other Swedish volunteers, Lars and Sven, and we met up regularly to download, relax and enjoy a little nightlife and a dinner free of the ubiquitous millet and cassava served in the bush. In Dar es Salaam we cruised around recklessly on our 50cc mopeds and feasted in unpromising hole-in-the wall food stalls in the market, where the West Indians ladled *dahl* and *chappati* onto shared platters from which we ate with our hands. I once had a nasty moped crash that landed me in the emergency room to remove glass from my face and eyes, but not once did I have any adverse effects from those dodgy lunches in the market, which I looked forward to for weeks when I was back in the bush.

One weekend, I left Mloka for some R&R in the city with a 3.5-meter long dead boa constrictor in the back of my land rover. The boa had found its way under my bed the day before, causing the biggest uproar I had ever seen in quiet Mloka. I had wanted to save the skin, so I convinced one of the men in the village to help me drag the 3-meter long monster to the river to drown it. Then I threw it in the land rover and resolved to deal with it in the city. But upon arrival in Dar es Salaam, I got waylaid by the invitation from my fellow Swedes to a round of beers and then another. It had been a long drought, and I confess I was out late – while my dead boa constrictor waited harmlessly in a plastic bag in the refrigerator of our apartment. I awoke at 4am to the shrieks of Sven who had apparently stayed out even later than I. When he opened the fridge for a cold drink of water, forty pounds of snake slithered out as if alive. I skinned the half-rotten beast the next day, much to the chagrin of my flatmates. I got a similar reaction some months later when I left the severed head of a warthog, a fascinatingly ugly beast with valuable tusks, soaking in the bathtub.

Shuttling between Mloka and Dar es Salaam, a day and a half long journey in the best conditions, was like a double dose of culture shock. Having finally acclimated to the austerity and deprivation of the bush, I could be eating lobster Thermidor the next day in Dar es Salaam, a teeming, cosmopolitan metropolis that had already afforded its version of culture shock. But I never tired of the contrast. The obstacles I faced that year, whether it was helping to transport a village out of the path of a herd of elephants or a load of sheet metal across a flooded road, were all part of my education in gaining two indispensible qualities for humanitarian work – regional resourcefulness and cultural curiosity.

THE RIFT VALLEY OF TANZANIA is the world's third largest mountain chain and the home of Mount Kilimanjaro, the highest free-standing peak in the world. I got it into my head that my trip to Tanzania would not be complete without scaling Kilimanjaro, and in the spring of 1970, I took a weeklong leave from the village to tackle this dream. With very little planning or equipment, a fellow volunteer named Torsten and I set off for the base of the mountain. After renting some basic equipment and the services of a local guide, we joined a group of five other climbers and began our ascent.

Towards the end of our fifth day of climbing, my friend began to suffer from altitude sickness. The air was very thin at 4,500 meters altitude and even after we rested in base camp, I could hear him gasping for breath. He was gaunt and ill. After a cold and harrowing night, Torsten turned back along with three others. I was left with one hearty American businessman of Swedish descent named Erling Lagerholm and our guide. On the last leg of the summit, we broke camp at 1am to make the top by sunrise. Kilimanjaro is a dormant volcano, and as we neared the top, we began to slide on the slippery combination of volcanic sand and snow. It was hard and slow going, and the sweat of our efforts froze the moment we stopped moving; that's how cold it was. At the top we were met with a blizzard that fully hid the sunrise. By then we were all suffering from oxygen deprivation in the bitter cold. Our thoughts and actions had become erratic, but not in an amusing way. There was no euphoria – only anti-climax and anxiety.

The exhilaration of tackling Mount Kilimanjaro and reaching its summit was severely delayed. It was not until I was back at the base of the mountain, nursing sweet milky tea that I acknowledged my achievement. When the recognition that I had vanquished the mountain finally dawned on me, it felt awfully good. I have never taken such joy in a cup of tea as I did in that dark, musty shack at the bottom of the mountain. Hours later, on the road home, I turned and looked back at the majestic mountain. I was filled with a deep and humbling gratitude. My pride in my accomplishment softened into a reverence for the powerful forces of nature that certainly could have been my undoing.

A YEAR AND A HALF HAD PASSED since my arrival in Mloka. I had become an honorary member of the village, a witness to deaths and births, and a participant in celebrations of all kinds. Mloka had fully embraced me and taught me invaluable lessons. The time had come to repay the village and I looked forward to unveil the great gift I had helped prepare. We arranged a small ceremony and turned on the taps of our finished water tower. I gave the cup to the village elder, a man with whom I had drunk tea many mornings since the last rainy season. He was to have the honor of the first drink from our tower. He took the cup skeptically and brought it to his lips. He took a swig and spit it out. "Bitter," he pronounced. He handed the cup to the medicine man, who tasted the chlorinated water and promptly put a curse on it.

My neighbors shook their heads and patted me on the shoulders, assuring me that it was ok that my water was bitter; there was plenty in the river, after all. They turned and made their way back to their huts, their lives and their river. The celebration was over, but I was the only one who saw it as a failure. For a moment I didn't full understand the ramifications of this rejection. The village leader had failed to endorse my project. It would never be used. In a decade the tower, the fruit of my efforts, would be a relic.

Today, of course, providing safe clean drinking water is an objective not just of the UN and its development agencies, but also for thousands of NGOs and grassroots organizations. Water-borne illnesses account for 1,400 deaths every day among children under five and contribute to impoverishment and poor health in communities everywhere. UNICEF has provided access to drinking water to more than 2 million people since 1990, and won't stop until the 750 million people worldwide who still lack safe drinking water can join the fortune. But acknowledging and addressing the so-called world water crisis is a full-time job in itself. It takes education and advocacy – not just to secure the support of donors, but also to secure the support of the beneficiaries. Without the buy-in of its stakeholders, no project, however lofty its aims and however well funded its operations, will succeed. Without the input of the people whose lives you plan to change, there can be no sustainable change.

I understood this only long after the village chief of Mloko retreated to the shade of his hut. No one had asked the villagers of Mloko what they needed to become a more "economically just, classless and collective" village. If someone had asked, he might have learned that seed or fertilizer or tools would have been a more useful offer. I had thought that the water tower would be an even more fundamental change in their lives; but when I left the village for the last time, the women who waved goodbye were back at the river, washing their clothes, filling their jerry cans, and, no doubt, conferring about the medicine man's curse on the water from the shiny tower.

On my final trip back to Dar es Salaam, I carried in the back of my vehicle a giant urn given to me by the villagers as a parting gift. It was a massive clay vessel used for holding water. I knew that it was meant as a symbol of their love, even if I couldn't help interpret it as a rebuke. This was *their* water tower – handed down through generations and made from the soil of the earth. I had tears in my eyes as I accepted it. As I drove away, it was perfectly clear to me that I was leaving Mloka with far more than I had given it.

It would be nearly fifteen years before I returned to Africa. When I did, I would dedicate another fifteen to her people as a servant of the United Nations. I am confident now, after decades of international service, that

I have settled my debt to Mloka. But I still identify with the concerns of young people eager to make lasting contributions to the world outside their own. My niece Claire has just completed a stint with the American Peace Corps on the Senegal/Mauritania border. This is a tough environment in which to bring any sort of effort to fruition, and Claire has made a go of it. Still, when we recently sat with a glass of wine to reflect on her experience, Claire expressed real reservations about whether she had "made a lasting impact." Wise beyond her years, Claire understands that the maternal health clinic she helped set up may well fall into disuse given the scarcity of doctors, transportation and any budget to speak of.

"I walked away the richer one," she said of the unwritten contract between the Peace Corps volunteer and the community she was dispatched to serve.

"It's ok to get more than you give," I told her. I believe this. I can already see the impact Claire will make in the next decade, all of it fuelled by the lessons she has learned while making a concerted, if not lasting, effort in a different environment. "It will even out in the end."

In Tanzania I learned to take nothing for granted. I learned to respect local customs and to appreciate the daily struggle for survival. I shed tears when I left, and I am not an emotional softie. Today, I really couldn't care less that the village of Mloka didn't need my water tower; I carted that enormous clay water jug home with me, and I glued its many pieces back together when it shattered in transit. I still cherish it - a symbol of my first taste of Africa, when I was a young man cutting my teeth on its challenges and relishing the softness of its true grit.

TOP Bjarred Primary School, 1957. The author is seated, furthest on the left.
BOTTOM The M/S Argentina freighter.

TOP LEFT The author as Platoon Commander of UNFICYP deployment to Famagusta.

TOP RIGHT In the Rufiji District, Tanzania, 1975. This record-breaking wildebeest was later eaten by the villagers of Mloka.

BOTTOM With shipmates on board the HMS Argentina during the 1962 embargo. The author is on the far right.

TOP On the tarmac at Phnom Phenh's Pochentong airport, 1975.

BOTTOM The UNICEF staff in Phnom Phenh at a local colleague's wedding. The author is standing on the far right. UNICEF Representative Paul Ignatieff is in the back row on the far left.

TOP Visit to Phnom Phenh by UNICEF Deputy Director, Charles Egger and his wife. Sami Behran is on the far left.

BOTTOM Aerial view of the Nong Samet refugee camps on the Thai/Cambodia border, established by UNICEF and ICRC.

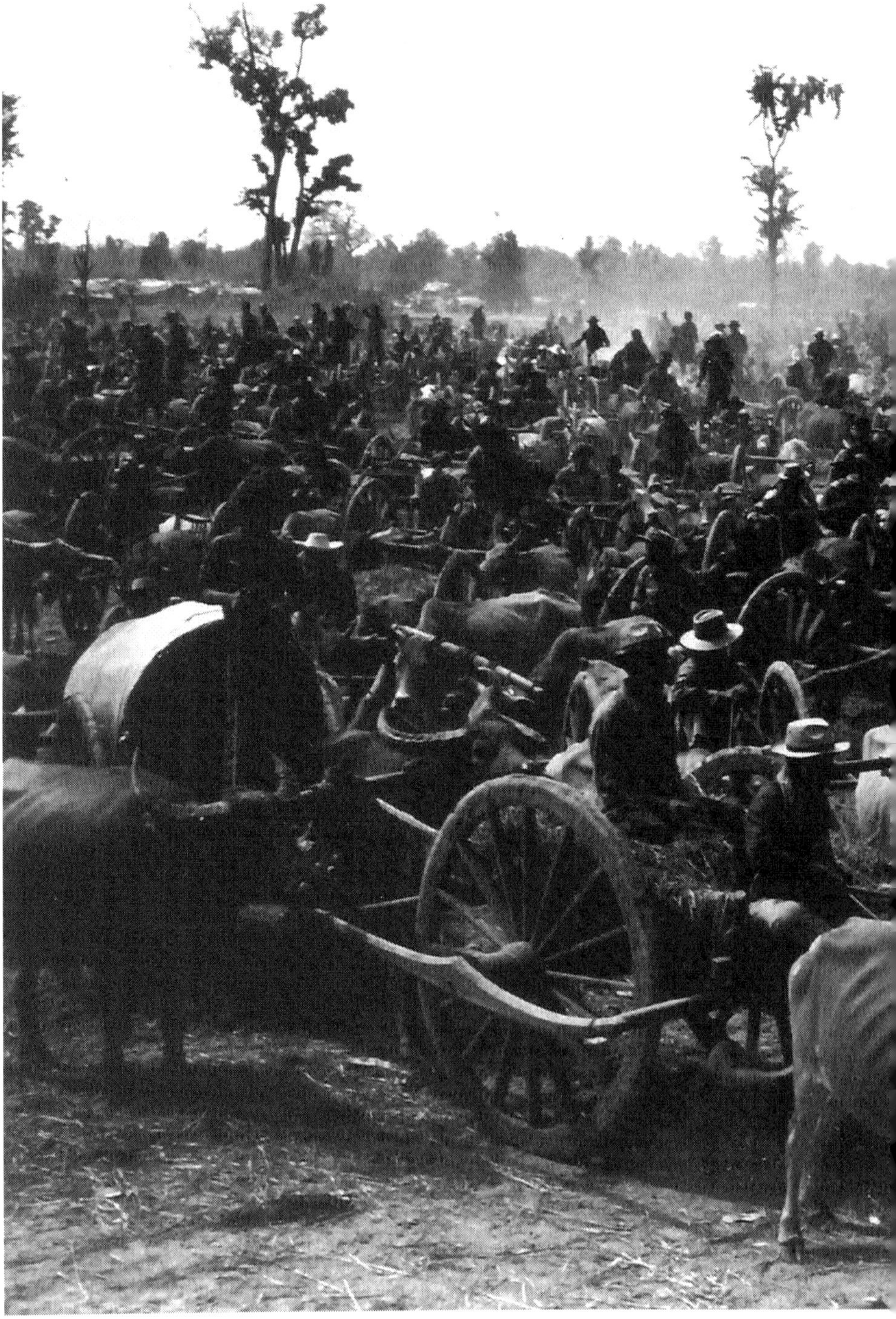

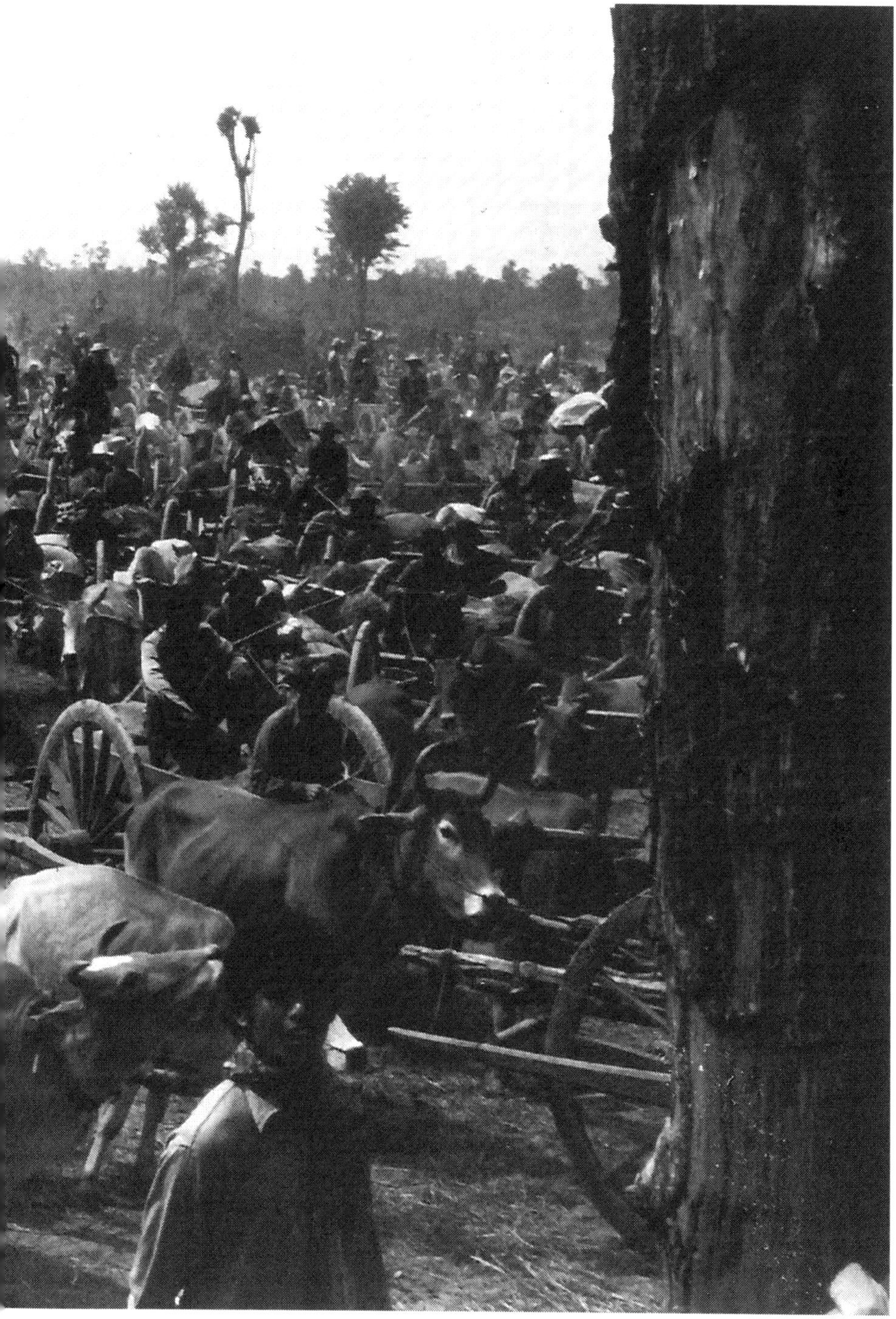

PREVIOUS PAGE The Land Bridge transporting seed, farm implements and hope back into Cambodia.
TOP The author with Queen Silvia and King Carl Gustav of Sweden (in white with glasses) visiting Khao i Dang Refugee Camp in 1981.
BOTTOM The author in Nong Chen camp during the Land Bridge distribution.

TOP The author with border refugee camp leaders in 1979. Van Seran of Mak Moun camp is on the left.

BOTTOM The author with, left to right, UN Secretary General Kurt Waldheim, Sir Robert Jackson, and Foreign Minister Sithi of Thailand. Aranyaprathet, 1980.

TOP UNICEF Executive Director Jim Grant shaking hands with Chadian dictator Hassan Habré.

BOTTOM The author joins Hassan Habré's forces on top of a captured Libyan tank after the battle at Faya Largeau.

TOP The author with local health practitioners in Mao, Chad during a vaccination campaign.

BOTTOM One of the solar-panel camel convoy bringing vaccinations to the desert in Chad.

LIBYA

CHAD

SUDAN

SOUTH
SUDAN

ETHIOPIA

SOMALIA

KENYA

TANZANIA

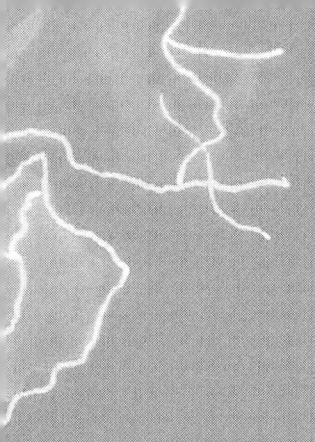

PART 3

CHILD SURVIVAL

CHAPTER 13

Ethiopia

MY THREE-YEAR TENURE IN ARANYAPRATHET left me with the reputation of a man who knew his way around a refugee camp. The complexities of providing aid in an arena distracted by politics and conflict demand a peculiar skill set that, by the early 1980's, was the essence of my professional resume: *experienced distributor of massive relief and practitioner of bush diplomacy, skilled in crowd control, logistical efficiency and sanity under stressful conditions.*

So when the time came for the Cambodian border camps to pass from UNICEF's control into the more mechanized hands of the World Food Programme, the head of WFP had a single condition: "Kristofferson's team stays on." So we did. We stayed on for another six months, long enough to facilitate the transfer of an enormous operation from one UN agency to another. The truth was that by mid-1982, I was close to losing that most valuable of my skills – my sanity. Eroded by relentless pressure and constant stress, my judgment had become clouded, my patience had thinned, and my fuse had grown far too short. I was, quite simply, on the brink of emotional and physical collapse.

Worse, I had neglected my family for three years. Seng Pheth and my two daughters had moved to Bangkok while I was in Aranyaprathet, and though we were close enough to spend weekends together, those weekends were too often cut short by an urgent summons back to the border.

I felt I had been a key player in helping tens of thousands of Cambodian families start new lives, but the time had come for a duty station that would allow me to be a father and husband to my own family.

We settled in Geneva, where the sheer orderliness of society threatened to give me vertigo. After the constant press of humanity that was my every waking breath in Aranyaprathet, the detached civility with which the good citizens of Geneva interacted struck me as something more profound than mere cultural difference. This was a society out of touch with survival, and hence – living in another state of mind altogether. Equally discomfiting was the prospect of deskwork in an office that felt as far removed from the beneficiaries of its efforts as NASA's mission control must feel from the moon. I knew full well that the lifesaving work that the organization does in the field would be impossible without the routine business of desk officers in the orderly headquarters. But my transition to Geneva was as philosophical as it was physical.

Though I could not verbalize the effect that this detachment had on me personally, it wasn't long before it was spelled out in no uncertain terms for me compliments of a Swiss gendarme. A few weeks into my new position I took some visiting friends into Zermat, a pretty Alpine town, for a Saturday lunch. Too accustomed to the off-road approach of life in southern Asia and involved in some discussion with my passengers, I blithely ignored road signs in four different languages ordering me to park my car and instead, chauffeured my guests straight into a pedestrian stretch of the town. The stern gendarme who stopped my vehicular trespassing was preparing a hefty fine for me when I mentioned to him that I was a UN employee, in the hopes he might be lenient. "I no care United Stations," was his curt reply. I often think of this unimpressed gendarme, particularly when my expectations for the organization I have served so long rise rise to untenabe heights. There are times, in moments of much needed humility, when "I no care United Stations," is a good mantra. Though the earnest and somber truth is that I care about the United Nations very much indeed.

I HAD BEEN APPOINTED DEPUTY CHIEF of UNICEF's Office of Emergency Programmes. My responsibility was to craft the agency's response to any crisis that should arise anywhere in the Middle East and Africa. There was no shortage of them in the early 1980's—from an earthquake in Turkey to civil war in Lebanon. But the most serious threat to women and children in the region was the drought sweeping across northern Africa. In many of the worst affected countries, violent conflict compounded the disaster of failed harvests. Famine was a specter across the continent, from Mauritania to Djibouti. In Ethiopia, it was very real.

The world did not become fully aware of the horrors of the Ethiopian famine until 1985, in large part thanks to the splashy advocacy of Bob Geldof's Live Aid concerts. Today, such celebrity-driven benefits are part and parcel of every disaster of international impact. The campaign is branded, the musicians are quick to sign up, and SMS channels for donating money to disaster victims flash across the jumbotron as seamlessly as the spotlights. But thirty years ago, an international concert to raise funds for disaster victims was still a novel idea. George Harrison's Concert for Bangladesh had tested the waters in 1971.

Geldof's Live Aid concert, billed as a "global jukebox," dwarfed its forefather in donations. Broadcast live from Philadelphia and London simultaneously, the concert for Ethiopia raised over $280 million dollars for famine relief and, less helpfully, made "We Are the World" and "Do They Know It's Christmas?" worldwide pop anthems. Geldof and his cohort of rock stars - including Led Zeppelin, Queen, The Who and U2 – would themselves have remained ignorant about the crisis in Ethiopia if not for the pioneering work of the remarkable photojournalist Mohammed Amin. A native Kenyan who rose from a modest background to become the most famous photographer in Africa, Amin covered every major event on the continent. I met him in Addis Ababa in 1985.

Amin's images of heartbreaking despair and human fragility in Ethiopia's starving camps that launched an international outcry. Amin, a fearless and ubiquitous presence in Ethiopia, would lose his arm in an explosion in 1991 while covering civil unrest in the country; he lost his life five years later while attempting to wrest control of a hijacked jet from terrorists who ultimately crashed the craft off the coast of the Comoros Islands.

But before there was Mo Amin with his video camera, and before there was Live Aid and "We are the World," there was just a silent emergency in which nearly one million people would die – most of them in an arid unsheltered wilderness, brutally exposed to the punishing conditions of the worst famine in a century. Their plight was particularly piteous because they were double victims. They were made hungry by failed crops and harvests but they were made helpless by a government that chose to ignore and, later, to exploit their hunger to maintain political power. UNICEF was instrumental in bringing the silent emergency to the forefront. But the organization that made its priority saving women's and children's lives did so in Ethiopia at the cost of being associated with a cruel dictator's less humanitarian agenda. Faced with the reality of women and children dying in ever-increasing numbers, it is my belief that we had no choice. The entities that struggled to provide relief in Ethiopia – UNICEF included – were battling government manipulation and misinformation as much as they were battling disease and malnutrition.

PRESIDENT MENGISTU HAILE MARIAM, the head of the Derg junta that overthrew Emperor Haile Selassie in 1974, was a committed Marxist and client of the Soviet Union. Mengistu's political ideology made him anathema to western governments, but it was his chauvinism and revolutionary fervor that proved disastrous for his people. His first act upon seizing power was to institute a reign of terror in which as many as 500,000 opponents were killed, including hundreds of children whose corpses were left to litter the streets of Addis Ababa.

Ten years later, as insurrections still flared, Mengistu viewed the natural disaster that threatened his people as another counterrevolution. "We must unite to liberate agriculture from the threatening forces of nature, …" he thundered in a speech given to mark his regime's tenth anniversary. Then he promised that the drought would be fought with "revolutionary determination."

That determination included the forced relocation of 1.5 million Ethiopians, often under conditions that can only be described as atrocities, from the northern famine regions to camps in the south. The resettlements began in November 1984 and continued until early 1986, sometimes undertaken without warning, preparation or willingness by the people who were being resettled. There were reports of families separated; of settlers essentially plucked from the food distribution lines and put on trucks requisitioned from the UN and international NGOs for human transfers. The camps to which the people were taken were utterly unsuitable for habitation. A government official from the relief commission conceded that the resettlement programme was often equated with the Soviet Gulag.

Mengistu's forced relocations sparked a bitter debate among humanitarian actors, some of whom saw the government's use of food aid as a bait-and-switch, a pretext for deportation, and ultimately a weapon of war. UNICEF, aware of the allegations of human rights abuses, quietly worked to redress the more egregious examples of enforcement while ensuring that its own presence in the country was not compromised by overtly anti-governmental lobbying.

The French NGO, Medecins Sans Frontieres, was the only aid organization to publicly denounce the programme and was promptly evicted from the country for its stance. This decision —brave but ultimately self-defeating — was a clear example of the moral dilemma that is inherent to many UNICEF programmes and which both Henry Labouisse and his successor, Jim Grant, had determined to shelve in order to ensure that women and children in the most dire of predicaments have a provider of last resort.

"We don't like the President, so the kids don't get immunized?" was Grant's standard response to detractors who recoiled from his willingness to shake with brutal dictators or military juntas. "You want to wait to launch the campaign until all governments are respectable?" The certainty that UNICEF had no right to place conditions on governments was a tenet of a much larger and more revolutionary shift that Grant orchestrated as Executive Director: the unconditional prioritization of child survival, above all other goals.

Grant's ability to deliver a tongue-lashing while simultaneously keeping mum on issues that might prove to be deal-breakers set a precedent for a longer policy that has allowed the organization to continue its work where other aid agencies cannot. It allowed UNICEF to continue work in Cambodia even with Khmer Rouge cooperation; to open the first humanitarian office in North Korea; and, long after Grant's death, to stay behind in Darfur in 2009 when a dozen other aid agencies were expelled by the

Sudanese government. This is an important legacy; UNICEF continues to enjoy a privileged trust with governments, allowing it to provide relief in conflict zones from which other organizations are forced out as unwanted witnesses or critics. Ethiopia's famine of 1983-1985 was an important case study in balancing human rights and humanitarian priorities.

THERE WERE WARNINGS of the coming famine as early as 1982, well before Mengistu embarked on his resettlement response. (Indeed, before the Ethiopian President was even willing to concede that there was any need for any government response to the conditions within his country.)

In March of that year, I was dispatched from Geneva as part of a UNICEF task force assigned by the Secretary General to assess the situation in northern Ethiopia, where the drought was worst and malnutrition most prevalent. I was assigned to Gondar province in the northwest. From Addis Ababa, the capital, we drove for hours through an arid wasteland, the monotony of which very nearly drove my objective from my mind until it manifested itself in a sudden, dizzying sight: tens of thousands of people lining the horizon. The first wave of a massive exodus out of the dry lands of Tigre and Wollo had crested before my vehicle.

Exiting the SUV, I faltered with an intense déjà vu. My ears rang with the same frightening silence of despair that I had experienced my first day on the border at Aranyaprathet. In the vast plain, broken only by shelters of sticks, rocks, and tall bushes, there was no human noise aside from the small sounds of death. There was no moaning or crying, for the women, children and old people were too exhausted for such exertion. The sun-bleached landscape was devoid of colour; there was not a spot of green anywhere in sight. But here and there were short punctuations of white: the bodies of the dead wrapped in respectful shrouds. Vultures circled above in the punishing sky.

Speaking to the refugees, we learned the worst: More than half of the population of the three northern provinces was on foot. More astonishing – they had nowhere to go. We knew from our own journey on the road north that there was no refuge, no relief, and no infrastructure to mark the end of these suffering souls' quest for another 150 kilometers.

We returned to Addis Ababa and alerted Grant to the situation. He was on the next plane out. We all knew the intransigence and indifference of Mengistu to his people. Convincing him of his duty to provide for them would be a tough sell, and Jim Grant was our best salesman. The UNICEF representative in the country, a woman referred to universally with deep respect as Madame Padmini, secured an audience with Mengistu to discuss UNICEF's concerns. To my amusement, the Marxist strongman received us at the former royal palace, seated on the former royal throne. The visit was short – shorter even than Mengistu, who struck me as a cruel, wizened man. Grant informed His Excellency that one thousand Ethiopians were dying every day because of his neglect. Mengistu retorted that there was no emergency in Ethiopia.

This was not an unexpected or even unusual response for the head of the famished country to make. A decade earlier, the emperor Haile Selassie had also rejected international concern, a contemptuous reaction to bad news that might sully his royal reputation. When UNICEF documented widespread famine conditions in 1973, the Vice Minister of Planning responded: "If we have to describe the situation in the way you have in order to generate international assistance, then we don't want that assistance. The embarrassment to the government isn't worth it. Is that perfectly clear?" Indeed, the Emperor's failure to recognize the enormity of the crisis and to tackle it accordingly largely ensured his overthrow by Mengistu's revolutionary communists, who were now buckling under the same denial.

Jim Grant's forthright nature allowed him to cede semantics to win the battle. Determined to save young lives, Grant simply acknowledged that UNICEF was requesting access to provide relief for this "non-emergency." He drove home the bargain by implying that shrewder Presidents than Mengistu bolstered their rule by providing generously for their nation's children. Paternalism, he hinted, is more powerful than all the revolutionary fervor under the sun. Mengistu, a wily opportunist, agreed. My sedentary life in Geneva was upended, and I was thrust headlong back into the daily grind of upping the odds of human survival

I spent five weeks in the autumn of 1982 helping the UNICEF office in Addis Ababa set up an emergency response to the famine. Much of this time was spent shuttling the 100 kilometer drive to Gondar over rugged mountains and, unless undertaken well before dawn, under a merciless sun. Halfway between Addis and Gondar was a small roadside café. Here, three hours into my journey, I made it my habit to stop for a daybreak breakfast of fried eggs and tea. Only once did I break this routine – by following the example of another regular, a local who came in and ordered a glass of something that he then mixed with a spoonful of ground chili and drank with relish. I very nearly died from this morning bracer, which seemed to affect the elderly gentleman not at all. I asked him what the hell I was drinking and why, and he told me it was tej, a potent alcoholic drink of fermented honey. "You drink it for health," he shrugged and then added that he was ninety-five years old and had drunk a glass of tej with a soupspoon of dried chili every day of his life.

As UNICEF continued its operations within Ethiopia with Mengistu's ostensible cooperation, my colleague to the west in Khartoum, the energetic UNICEF Representative Samir Basta, was becoming concerned about the exodus of Ethiopians out of the northern Tigre region into Sudan. As many as 3,000 people were crossing the border every day, they said, desperate for food. UNICEF assessments in Tigre, a province in open revolt against Mengistu's forces, found spiking rates of child malnutrition and rampant epidemics among the rebel population. There was no choice but to intervene. Naturally, the operation had to be kept covert if we wanted to maintain our presence throughout Ethiopia and avert a wider famine. By this time, the Tigrean People's Liberation Front was allied with the Eritrean People's Liberation Front to topple the regime.

We considered the precarious position of working both sides of a geopolitical flashpoint and deferred to the UNICEF Sudan representative, Samir Basta. He agreed with my assessment of the stakes and proceeded to set up a direct, personal channel for me to communicate with armed militants, a situation that the UN generally avoided and always denied.

There was no way for our negotiating team to reach rebel-held Tigre from within Ethiopia. Instead we flew from Khartoum to Port Sudan and travelled south through the interior into the mountains. These were stealthy runs made under cover of night with nothing but the breath of our pack horses to lead us over narrow mountain paths to the no-man's land on the border. There, in the ruins of a shell-shocked house and by the light of a kerosene lamp, I sat down with members of the Tigrean Liberation Force to sketch out a supply route. The relief chain of pack mules and smugglers would traverse rugged mountains by night, when the bombers of the Ethiopian Air Force fell silent. Our negotiations with the rebels took place over two days, during which my initial awe of the beauty and fierceness of the insurgents – men and women who had been trained to fight since birth – gave way to profound respect and solidarity. In the end, the emergency corridor we helped open, managed to supply women and children with lifesaving supplies for about six months, until control of the area shifted once more and the population emerged from its siege.

DROUGHT AND HUNGER, tragically, are still cyclical realities in the Horn of Africa in the 21st century. Since the famine of 1983, there have been five droughts and hunger scares in the region. In late 2011, the region bore a triple-threat: the worst drought in decade; a spike in food prices; and violent conflict. As a result, hunger and malnutrition were pandemic, prompting another enormous humanitarian operation to assist more than 13 million affected people. It was a qualified success. Thirty years after the Ethiopian famine, the number of international NGO's with experienced emergency staff has grown exponentially, along with the means of building awareness and donations through social media and advocacy. But even as the speed of information helps catalyze emergency response, we remain, in the United Nations, stymied by the same obstacle: sovereignty. UN personnel cannot – MAY not – respond to a need until the government in question asks for assistance. Yet heads of state continue to deny or dismiss the need for international aid.

In 2012, the President of Ethiopia, Meles Zenawi, ignored warnings of a looming catastrophe and refused to acknowledge the severity of the situation. Worse, Zenawi managed to pervert the way the international community speaks about famine, which is now relegated to a quasi-scientific ranking of "food security." Virtually all humanitarian organizations now speak this euphemized language of "shortage" and "malnutrition," in an effort to appease host governments and ensure that they be allowed access to feed the very people whose misery is being denied.

But no one, I would venture, used food and food aid as a weapon of war as effectively as Mengistu Mariam. For his crimes were not limited to stalling tactics. They continued even after we arrived, too late to save thousands but still in time to save tens of thousands. Every day, I and everyone in the community of international civil servants around the world, had to make our peace with henchmen and bandits who take food from the mouths of babes and line their pockets with the world's generosity. But Mengistu's criminal use of the most fundamental humanitarian endeavor as a pretext for political repression leaves a taste in my mouth more intolerable than tej. It's a very good thing that UNICEF has an excellent track record of putting "cooler heads" in charge of delicate operations. For there is no denying, it is an organization that must rise above a great deal of hideous human behavior to save human lives.

CHAPTER 14

Sahel

IN 1985, I WAS CONTACTED BY THE UNICEF Regional Director Bertram Collins. who offered me a position as a country representative. I had mixed feelings about my new duty post – Chad was a particularly challenging, war-torn nation. But it was a country where the efforts of UNICEF's back-to-basics approach to reducing child mortality would have a palpable impact. I accepted the offer.

Jim Grant, a second-generation internationalist who dedicated his life to development and humanitarian activism, was the third man to hold the directorship of the United Nations Children's Fund. Lauded by many for his vision, leadership and commitment, Jim was, undeniably, larger than life. He was appointed to the position by the Secretary General on the suggestion of U.S. President Jimmy Carter, who likely related to Grant's missionary zeal. In the fifteen years he served the agency, Grant revolutionized UNICEF's strategy by identifying a single goal as superior to all other objectives in the broad mandates of the charter: child survival.

Grant looked at the causes of the estimated 14 million annual deaths of children under age five – malnourishment, preventable diseases, and waterborne illnesses – and saw only preventable causes of death. This, he said, was a scandal. "The equivalent," he quipped, "of 120 jumbo jets full of kids crashing daily, and no one noticing." UNICEF, he asserted, was capable of reaching all of these children, not just the thousands that its scattered offices could easily target. With a laser focus on vaccination, breastfeeding, growth monitoring and oral rehydration treatment for diarrheal disease, Grant directed UNICEF to save five million young lives immediately. Vaccination rates, he insisted, would need to double in five years and double again in ten. He doubled the agency's budget, quadrupled its field staff and achieved his objective. UNICEF's success in reducing the under-five mortality rate from 40,000 deaths per day to less than 20,000 deaths per day in just one generation is Jim Grant's legacy. It was, in the words of Grant and everyone who has attempted to characterize the revolution he executed in a heavily bureaucratized organization "a quantum leap" in child survival.

It was a leap that required significant investment and found significant opposition - initially. The scope of Grant's vision flew in the face of the very real absence of money, political will and even roads in the places he hoped to affect his revolution. Some of his veteran staff balked. I did not. This, after all, was the man whom I first met at the Cambodian border where he asked me how much money I needed to supply my Land Bridge farmers with the tools to replant Cambodia. I told him $20 million, and he told me to "think bigger." So it was no surprise to me to that our new Director was thinking big on the biggest of topics: UNICEF's very mission.

If Jim Grant was a man with a vision, he was also a man who liked visual cues. He carried a talisman wherever he went. It represented UNICEF's faith in simple, affordable child survival, and it fit in the pocket of his suit jacket. Whether he was meeting health ministers in Africa, tribal leaders in Afghanistan, school teachers in China or the Pope in his chambers, the first thing the UNICEF director extended after his big glad hand was a sachet of oral rehydration salts. At $0.08 a dose, ORS was the symbol of Grant's single-focus mission to reduce the number of preventable child deaths, and it went everywhere with him as his inanimate spokesperson.

But Jim had another favorite prop in his ever-changing rotation – one that, for a time, became an iconic image of UNICEF's ubiquitous presence. It was a photograph that I took while I was the UNICEF representative in Chad, and it showed a convoy of camels about to embark on an historic mission.

Chad is a landlocked country divided by three climate bands. The capital, N'Djamena, is in the southern savannah; in the middle of the country is the arid belt called Sahel; and the northernmost region is a sparsely populated strip of the Sahara desert. At the time of my posting, in the mid 1980s, the desert was slightly more crowded than usual: Thousands of Libyan fighters had crossed the border and occupied a significant stretch of the desert. An equivalent number of French legionnaires, invited by the government in N'Djamena, faced off with these rebel invaders at the 16th parallel. The Libyans were taking advantage of twenty years of civil strife in Chad to press Muammar Qaddafi's expansionist agenda. The French were there to take advantage of any pretext to strike back at Tripoli

UNICEF had to contend with all these desert forces in order to pursue its own interest in the Sahara – the Gorans, who, though among the largest migratory ethnic group in the world are, nonetheless, hard to reach when surrounded by bristling warlords and endless sand dunes.

Shortly after my arrival in N'Djamena, we began to hear reports of a terrible measles epidemic among the Gorans. Children were dying quickly and in large numbers. The solution – an immediate vaccination drive to halt transmission – would have been easy in a well-developed suburb, a rural area with a few rough roads, or even a densely populated slum. But to bring the measles vaccine, which must be maintained at a constant temperature across the desert, without a source of electricity, was a challenge.

As I surveyed the northern territories, I recalled a disastrous decision I had made some years before when I elected to travel from Bamako, Mali to Dakar in Senegal overland – that is, through the desert of Mauritania. On that journey our vehicle flipped in a sand dune and my driver and I found ourselves deep in the Sahara in the middle of the night with a disabled jeep and a skin rash from the spilled diesel we carried with us. If it hadn't been for a hospitable encampment of nomads who welcomed us with balm for our burns and the finest cup of tea I have ever thanked the gods for, I wonder if we would have finished our trip alive.

As I thought back to that ordeal, I understood that the stakes in Chad were much higher. With children's lives on the line, I needed a more reliable supply chain than my skeleton staff and small fleet of jeeps could provide. And I needed a constant energy source to cross the desert as well.

The solution we came up with was trumpeted as "cutting edge" and the "newest innovation," but was, in its essence, utterly primitive. To create a cold-chain to northern Chad, we turned to ancient desert transportation and the most basic of energy sources: camels and the sun.

When we hit upon the idea in war-wrecked N'Djamena, solar panel technology was still in its earliest stages, and it took some international sleuthing to find a company in Finland that was able to produce panels to our specifications and, just as spectacularly, willing to donate them to our worthy cause.

As has been the case in much of my career, one of the people who was pivotal to this particular endeavor was a man with whom I had a history and with whom I would continue to work long after our camels became celebrities in the humanitarian world. Martti Ahtisaari was the Minister of the Finnish Development Cooperation at the time, but when Ube Lindstrom, the head of the UNICEF National Committee in Finland, introduced me to him, I laughed in recognition. Ahtisaari had been the Finnish Ambassador to Tanzania during my Peace Corps years, and we had met in Dar es Salaam some decades ago. When we met again Ahtisaari generously directed Finnish government funding towards our vaccination in Chad.

We kept in touch after this work as well, catching up over beers in Helsinki in his Finnish sauna. Ahtisaari even offered me a position in his cabinet as the UN Administrator of Namibia in the interim between its liberation from South African's apartheid government and first democratically elected government. I passed on this opportunity, as I was too invested in Operation Lifeline in Sudan, but my connection with Ahtisaari continued through his UN career and his rise to become the President of Finland. I consider him an outstanding individual. So does the Nobel committee, which awarded him the Nobel Peace Prize in 2008 for his conflict resolution work in Kosovo, Namibia, Indonesia and elsewhere.

On the day the Finnish-produced panels arrived at my office in N'Djamena, my colleague Bruno Gabrieli and I sequestered ourselves in the UNICEF garage. There was not exactly an abundance of corner hardware stores in the capital, so we plundered the UN mechanics' toolbox and got to work to design a portable refrigerator. Several days later we emerged with the least-cumbersome prototype of our efforts.

Next we set about purchasing our ungulate "fleet." I was just a Swede with a frequent flyer pass between New York, Geneva and the Horn of Africa limited. Some years prior to my assignment in Chad, I had spent three months in the desert outside Timbuktu, where I often camped under the stars in various Tuareg settlements. One such night I awoke to the sound of rain against a nearby tent flap and a light mist of precipitation on my cheek. I jolted upright to announce the arrival of a long-awaited rain. "Shhh, Kristofferson," came the bemused response of my comrade, Michel Siddibe. "It's the camels pissing." Today Siddibe is the Executive Director of UNAIDS. I don't know what has become of those camels.

My Chadian purchase agents returned with seven sturdy, ornery camels, and all were officially registered as UN vehicles with a tattooed license plate on their rump. Most of them endured the branding calmly enough. They were less patient when it came time to strap a bulky, shiny, fragile refrigerator to their backs. The shrieking brought the entire staff into the courtyard and not a lick of work got down that day.

The cold-chain camels made their maiden voyage in May 1985. We followed them much of the way to their destination but turned back when the desert overtook the highway. This mobile vaccination crew was part of a larger countrywide team that managed to bring the measles epidemic under control in a matter of months. Mission accomplished, we retired our valiant mobile health workers, thanking them for their service. By then we had realized that they had accomplished more than stopping measles in the desert; they had given UNICEF a massive marketing tool. Donations soared when the fundraisers saw the photos and videos of our marriage of new thinking and old tools. And Jim Grant was one of the camel's biggest champions.

Sadly, after its triumphant roll-out the camel convoy had less success. After my tenure as UNICEF Representative in Chad, no one stepped forward to lead the project or even, in the parlance of project management, to "own" it. Without a local team to care for the animals, UNICEF's stake in the operation faltered. My pet project had become just that. It is a shame that it was short-lived, but it is also a testament to the importance of individual entities and enthusiasms within a larger organization.

Meanwhile, we needed more than camels to ensure that our vaccination drive reached all of the children of Chad. We needed manpower and expertise. Neither of these was available to me in N'Djamena, where the primary preoccupation was war – both internal and external. Ideally, UNICEF's in-country support works with the existing government structure to enhance the state's own resources and systems. In addition to our regular interventions on behalf of children, we are tasked with what is called in technocrat-ese, "capacity building." This entails training in budget, staffing, and scheduling to allow developing countries to include child-welfare services in the growth of their economies and budgets. In Chad I was acting, for the first time, as the UNICEF Representative. As the highest-ranking officer in the country, it fell to me to impress upon the government authorities their responsibility to their youngest constituents. I didn't disregard this task; but I also understood the lay of the land. Realpolitik dictated that I rely on my own resources until there was real peace in the country.

So I called upon Guido Bertolaso, the eminent Italian doctor who had rushed to my side in Aranyaprathet with his skilled surgeons. I had never forgotten the skill and professionalism with which he and his team had treated the women and children who had traversed mine fields to escape the killing fields. Guido was now a high-ranking official in Italy, a minister of civil response, and he immediately agreed to send me a team of experienced field doctors.

Not long after, I stood at the airport, waiting for my latest recruits. As the Air Italia disgorged its passengers onto the blazing hot tarmac, I wondered which of them were my doctors and nurses. And then there emerged at the top of the stairs, two impossibly glamorous creatures in mini-skirts, windblown coiffures and décolletage. With an enormous grin on my face that I simply could not wipe off, I set about explaining the importance of following local customs. Vana and Renata, two of the finest nurses Italy has ever produced, heard me out on the subject of modest dress and conservative Muslim gender roles and rushed off to the market to update their wardrobe. Then, garbed in the flowing robes of their hosts, they headed into the desert, where they spent two years winning the hearts and minds of communities less impressed by their good looks than the French legionnaires stationed around the country.

Being UNICEF's representative in Chad was a job that rarely allowed me to futz about in the garage making lifesaving toys. Most of my time was taken up in meetings with the government officials whose cooperation was vital to UNICEF's progress in the country. With its economy diverted largely to military spending, Chad depended almost entirely on foreign aid for its health services. Deplorable as such priorities were, this dependence allowed UNICEF the opportunity to implement an ambitious scaled-up health system. Our goal was to strengthen basic service delivery at the village level by establishing health posts manned by trained community health workers. The scale of our ambitions meant that I spent as much time at the Ministry of Health as I did in my UNICEF offices.

But I knew from my early days in Tanzania with the Swedish Peace Corps that I needed to give as much or more of my personal attention to the power brokers far from N'Djamena. The country operated on parallel power structures – the government administration and the traditional tribal leadership network. If I were to secure the participation of the entire country in our expanded network of child services, I needed to win over the tribal leaders whose influence was, at least in territory, far greater than the central authority of the government.

For the first time in my UNICEF career, diplomacy took precedence over operational problem solving. And this was not the informal nod and wink bush diplomacy that I had become skilled at on the Thai border or in clandestine meetings with Tigre rebels. This was palace diplomacy, in which low bows and humble honorifics were absolutely essential.

Sultan Alifa Ali Zezerti was perhaps the most powerful of the tribal leaders. His fiefdom, called Mao, was located on the northeast shore of Lake Chad and stretched along the border with Niger, covering about one-eighth of the country. It was an area particularly exposed to epidemics because of its porous border. The Sultan's land was an absolute key target for our vaccination efforts. Like so many of the eminent men I have had the pleasure to work with in my life, the Sultan of Mao was huge. In his flowing white robes, he was always the center of activity in his palace compound, an unassuming concentration of bright white buildings in the middle of the desert. Though he spoke little French, we communicated easily with the help of a translator. The first of our visits began with a pleasant exchange about livestock - a topic of great importance to the Sultan. Again, I thanked my father for my modest husbandry knowledge. Then I turned the topic of conversation to children, specifically the thousands of children for whom he was king. Over the course of our relationship I met three of Sultan Alifa Ali's wives and more of his children and grandchildren. I never set foot in his vast territory without first paying my respects at his palace door.

When my three-year tenure in Chad was up, I made a point to say goodbye to the Sultan in person. I arrived to find that he had prepared a farewell banquet in my honor. All of the chiefs of the province were invited to this feast, the main course of which was an elaborate dish called *mischui*: a couscous-stuffed chicken cooked in a goat inside a camel. This remarkable banquet, with its music and dancing and kind words spoken by all, is an enduring memory of my work in Chad, as is the Sultan's parting gift: a beautiful snow white camel. I thanked Alifa Ali heartily, my hands clasping his. I furrowed my brow in concern over whether the streets of Manhattan, where I was next bound, would be kind to such a noble beast. Then I begged him, as a dear friend, to please take good care of the camel until I could return and carry it back to a more worthy home. My diplomacy had reached a level of courtliness.

Less smooth were my relations with Chad's official head of state, President Hissene Habré. Habré came to power in 1982 with significant assistance from the CIA and the Pentagon. Three years later, he had solidified his domestic authority with a campaign of terror and torture. His brutality, however, went unremarked by his western sponsors. Ronald Reagan had just declared a war on terror; Habré's fight with the world's best-known terrorist, Muammar Qadaffi, trumped his crimes against his people.

When I arrived in Chad, Habré's forces had recently repulsed a Libyan advance on the capital, which still reeked of insecurity and fear. The arrival gate at the airport, for example, was ringed with abandoned military vehicles, and every window in the airport was blown out. In the oppressive heat I felt delirious and wondered if I had arrived back in Phnom Penh under siege. I spent the first week in the shambles of our office and in the looted Le Chadian hotel. Within weeks, the Libyan aerial bombardments began again. I awoke one night to find my ceiling in my bed.

Squeezed tight, Habré proved to be even more ruthless. His henchmen traveled the city in their signature Toyota trucks, conscripting young boys in broad daylight to fight the Libyans. It fell to me, as the voice of child protection, to demand a stop to these kidnappings. In truth, I can't be certain that any of my grim-faced declarations or condemnatory written statements on the subject helped to release even a single boy from forced conscription. It would take three decades, the passage of a dozen more Representatives through my old post, an international campaign to protect children from conflict, and the 2007 resolution by governments at an international summit in Paris dedicated to ending military recruitment of children, before Chad gave its commitment to demobilize its own child soldiers. By then, I fear, many young lives had already been stolen and turned over to the battlefield and to abuse. Sadly, the so-called Paris Principles - as meaningful and important as they are to international standards of child protection - are regularly violated even by states that have publicly adopted their disavowal of child recruitment. Today the indiscriminate nature of warfare against civilians is proving to be even bloodier for young people than the wars of the last century. UNICEF's child protection strategies are among the organization's most challenging. There are still many Habré's plaguing the world's children.

Aside from the quick meeting during which I presented my credentials to Habré as the UNICEF Representative, the only time I had an audience with this deplorable man was in the company of Jim Grant, who was doing the rounds of country offices in the Sahel. On our way to the meeting, I filled Jim in on the latest of the strongman's crimes. Two French nuns had recently been shot by the President's personal guards, and only one had survived. I told Grant this by way of introduction to what a nasty character we were on our way to meet. It never occurred to me that he would take it upon himself to rebuke the President. But sure enough, at the conclusion of our formal introduction, Grant brought up the nuns. Luckily, the translator refused to translate the question. Otherwise, I have no doubt UNICEF would have been booted from the country.

As in every duty station I had worked in to date, the geopolitical situation in Chad was far from conducive to humanitarian work. While I was there, I witnessed an enormous investment by the west in the country – an investment metered only in weapons and military training. In this respect, it would have been better in some ways if Chad had remained a neglected African state. That western support helped prop up a regime of unspeakable criminality. Habré is known as "Africa's Pinochet." The comparison goes beyond his well-documented use of torture and terror to hold onto power; Habré would ultimately earn the dubious distinction of being the first African dictator tried for crimes against his people. Ousted in a coup in 1990, the dictator fled to Senegal, where his ill-gained wealth provided him with a comfortable and secure exile for over a decade. He was indicted in 2000 and is currently awaiting trial for crimes against humanity, including the killing and systematic torture of civilians.

Meanwhile, despite its oil revenues, Chad remains the most impoverished country in central Africa. Child malnutrition is at emergency levels. Less than half of the nation's children are enrolled in school and only half of them will complete the primary grades. This widespread deprivation makes Chad vulnerable to the same Islamic elements that have destabilized the governments of Mali and Niger in recent years – fundamentalist forces and armed jihadists spun out of the chaos of Libya. Meanwhile, civil wars in Central African Republic and in South Sudan have sent half a million people into Chad looking for refuge. Their presence further taxes a government ill-equipped to provide for its people.

During my tenure as UNICEF Representative, I worked with an extraordinary team. Despite its insecurity and challenges, Chad in 1982 was the destinatioin selected as a first international post for a handful of brave young international development workers, most of them women. These dauntless and energetic women were welcomed and given invaluable support from a crew of courageous Chadians. We made a real impact in our short time together.

Today UNICEF in Chad continues our work. True to Jim Grant's word, the organization looks beyond the ineradicable obstacles – war, disaster, displacement and greed – to focus on the eradicable causes of death. In 2014, two million children in Chad were vaccinated against measles. Perhaps some of those vaccinations arrived by camel.

CHAPTER 15

Lifeline Sudan

BY LATE 1985, THE MASSIVE INFLUX of international attention and aid had staunched the famine fatalities in Ethiopia. But even as the situation improved in Ethiopia, another wave of drought and instability was cresting to the west. The Horn of Africa's tragic cycle dictated another emergency response. This time, ground zero was Sudan. And it fell to me, promoted to Chief of Emergency Operations in New York, to coordinate the extraordinarily expensive, multinational, multpronged Operation Lifeline Sudan (OLS).

I was a single man again. After 12 years of marriage, Seng Pheth and I agreed that my job and her domestic happiness were incompatible. Though she and my precious daughters would stay in my life, my professional promotion to UNICEF headquarters in New York was a move I made solo. I was excited about my new position and about being at the physical heart of the United Nations, but the country boy in me rebelled at the idea of going home to a cramped box in the sky. I was willing to put up with the crowds of Grand Central Station and Turtle Bay by day, but I hung my hat each night in a small ranch style house in the suburbs.

That winter was a cold one. As a Swede, I relished the snow and dark that I had often longed for while living in desert or monsoon zones. That winter, I got my fill of bracing weather while standing on the Metro North platform in New Rochelle. Every morning found me there at 6 a.m. in my long coat and shined shoes, blending in well with my fellow commuters. Except that I was the only one on the train without a newspaper folded open to the stock report; my morning reading was invariably dispatches from Khartoum, Addis Ababa and Nairobi. When I lifted my eyes from my briefcase to gaze out the window, it was not the marinas of Eastchester Bay and the rail-yards of the south Bronx I saw; It was the hard-cracked banks of the Blue Nile, the trackless Nuba mountains, the hot sun that produces sweat and suffering alike. My mind wandered far to Sudan, the country that I had first encountered while trying to fight famine and government neglect in neighboring Ethiopia.

The 6:12 am from New Rochelle arrived at Grand Central at 6:48. That got me to the door of Jim Grant's apartment on 38th street at 7 am sharp. Nearly a decade after we first met on the Cambodia/Thai border, circumstances now threw Grant and I together on a daily basis. Every morning during the winter of 1989, Jim's wife Edith met me at the door with a cup of coffee. She proffered that cup with a wink, as if to say, "Here's about one-tenth of what you will need to get you through the day, but I know you've got the rest covered." A few minutes later, Jim would emerge in his dressing gown and launch immediately into business.

Operation Lifeline Sudan was not a project close to Grant's heart. He had resolved long ago to avoid diverting the organization's resources and attentions with another massive emergency relief effort like the Cambodian border operation. Nonetheless, the UNICEF director had to comply with a request from Secretary General Perez de Cuelar to lead the mobilization of relief to Sudan, where the situation was so dire that even the warring factions were willing to cooperate to facilitate a humanitarian intervention.

Brokering cease-fires to complete thorough child vaccination campaigns is one of UNICEF's signature victories. Jim's unique combination of ego stroking and shaming laid the ground for these humanitarian cease-fires, beginning in El Salvador in 1985 and continuing today in conflict zones like Afghanistan, where UNICEF recently brokered a three-day cease-fire to vaccinate 1.4 million children against polio.

In 1989 Grant berated the armed militants of Sudan with the same question he had asked Ethiopia's Mengistu: "What sort of leader can't provide for his people's children?" Thus were born the corridors of peace that allowed UNICEF to provide food and supplies for millions of starving people.

Our daily work began with that first cup of coffee in the Director's apartment overlooking the East River. I reported the overnight intelligence, boiled down to a two-page summary as per Grant's request. He then gave his marching orders and Edith handed me my coat. On occasion, we would walk the three blocks to the UNICEF office together, still puzzling out the logistics of some fresh supply line or the diplomacy around a sensitive, urgent request.

During the two years that I helped coordinate UNICEF's emergency operation in war-torn Sudan, I watched Jim Grant in action as closely as anyone. I was one of a troop of Grant flank men during tense negotiations with hardened warlords and intractable Islamists, and I marveled at his energy, commitment and passion. But I also saw the sharp end of his personality – the fragility of his bonhomie and the selectivity of his candor. Jim Grant was an unstoppable dynamo, an inspiring leader and, yes, a bit of a "mad American" as many of his befuddled employees muttered, but he was never your friend. Jim was like a speeding bullet. If you were located on the trajectory of his bull's eye, you would feel his steely focus. If you were not on that trajectory, you were simply not on Jim's radar. I occupied many different positions while working in the Jim Grant administration of UNICEF. In 1989, I was speeding with him.

OPERATION LIFELINE SUDAN was the United Nations' finest solution to the riddle of how to provide impartial aid in a war zone through multiple relief agencies. Africa's largest country was well into the second phase of its protracted civil war when Lifeline was willed into existence. An earlier cease-fire accord had granted the southern third of the country – home to the country's ethnic and religious majority – some autonomy from Khartoum, the capital of the governing Islamic minority in the north. But the country lived on a narrow blade of conflict. In 1983 Khartoum reclaimed the south as part of an Islamic state and imposed *sharia* law. In response, the nascent Sudan People's Liberation Army (SPLA) took up arms in the name of persecuted non-Islamic Sudanese throughout the country. The fighting was bloody, indiscriminate and fractured; the northern forces rent by coups, the southern rebels split into factions that persist today – committing atrocities in the name of internecine conflict.

Meanwhile, the war had an additional fatal side effect – famine. By 1988, some 250,000 people had died of starvation, unaided because of the obstacles of fighting. With those deaths on our conscience, the international community resolved to establish a humanitarian lifeline protected by treaty from interference by warring factions. Established after lengthy negotiations between government and rebel factions, the OLS provided the diplomatic cover and operational support necessary to maintain humanitarian and food aid to the women and children caught in the middle of conflict. It was one of the first instances in which UNICEF was able to secure binding agreements promising to honor certain ground rules of neutrality to allow humanitarian workers to function, and was, as such, an unprecedentedly straightforward and principled structure.

Run simultaneously out of three hubs – the northern capital Khartoum; Juba in South Sudan; and Nairobi, Kenya – OLS was a massive operation, coordinating all the activities and resources of 35 NGO's plus the World Food Programme. UNICEF and the WFP were selected as lead agencies. It was a huge responsibility and as complex as running refugee camps on the Thai border. But as I was made familiar with the Lifeline structure and key personnel, I was reassured: Charles LaMuniere, a senior advisor to the UN Secretariat, had extensive famine experience; from Washington we had the support of Julia Taft of the American Office of Foreign Disaster Assistance and UN Ambassador Thomas Pickering; Brad Morse, head of UNDP and Jim Ingram, chief of WFP, were also enlisted; from UNICEF I had the firm backing of Jim Grant himself and the regional directors, Richard Reed in Ankara, M. Hossein in Khartoum, and Mary Racelis in Nairobi. Vincent O'Reilly, an old friend and colleague, would be my liaison in Nairobi. *How could we fail*, I thought with enthusiasm.

In fact, I would get the failures out of the way early. My first task was to get my boots on the ground and to join my colleagues in the field and assess the scope of our mission. I needed to know what resources, transportation, personnel and logistics we had at our disposal in southern Sudan, which was where the bulk of the suffering and need was. I spoke with Vincent, who had recently been relocated to Nairobi from Afghanistan, and we made a date.

It had been years since I had last seen Vincent, and we celebrated our reunion on the border post of Loki Chokio. There we were joined by the two Dutch pilots who were to fly us into the bush the following day. I made my exit from the bar at midnight, leaving Vincent and the pilots with a half-bottle of gin. Four hours later I had to wake them myself in order to make our scheduled departure time. I wondered if, in the state the pilots were in, I ought not ask Vincent to man the controls. In fact, we managed to crash no fewer than three planes that day – through no fault of the slightly hung-over pilots. The first crashed when the landing gear failed on landing in Kapoeta, in southern Sudan. The second and third planes both spluttered and resigned shortly after takeoff, leaving us to wonder if we would be staying the night in Kapoeta – a highly unattractive proposition given the level of fighting in the area. Only after a fourth small craft was dispatched to our aid did we successfully arrive back in Kenya. Four planes, and the assessment had been inconclusive. Our fly over south Sudan had given us no intelligence about the movements of people displaced by fighting. It had only given us headaches.

Eventually, after several more reconnaissance missions, we were able to get a clear picture of the challenges for OLS: The Lifeline would have to follow the Nile and be supported by a hefty investment from the UN to build a railroad into Sudan's remotest enclaves. But first, we needed to secure the agreement of the de facto head of southern Sudan. That was a man named John Garang, a Dinka – tall, dark and stately. He spoke in a deep bass - a commanding but intelligent voice. Garang had earned an economics degree in America and studied further in Dar es Salaam before returning to his homeland to join the rebels fighting for a unified, secular Sudan. When the first civil war ended, Garang was absorbed into the Sudanese national army, but at the first indication that peace was in jeopardy, he reinstated his rebel credentials to form the Sudanese People's Liberation Army (SPLA). Ironically, as Commander-in-Chief of the rebels, Garang was Sudan's best chance to forge national unity.

Garang made several trips to the United Nations and always met with

Jim Grant during his visit. I was present for several of those meetings, keeping a steady course between the two figures towering over me (and I am no small man). Though he was universally admired among the UNICEF officers who encountered him, Garang was a tough negotiator. He never shied from telling us if we did not see eye-to-eye. He never shrank from defending his cause by going toe-to-toe on any clause of our agreement, no matter how trivial. These negotiations in 1989 were nonetheless fruitful, and more rewarding than those we underwent with Garang's nemesis – Omar Hassan al-Bashir.

Al-Bashir had led the military coup that deposed the heads of state with whom we had worked to first establish Lifeline: President Ahmad al-Mirghani and his prime minister, Sadiq al-Mahdi. After the coup, al-Bashir revealed himself as a cold-blooded tyrant with a hot temper. In our negotiations with him, Jim Grant, Jim Ingram and I laid out the conditions that we had already negotiated with both Garang and al-Mighani. Al-Bashir responded with what can only be called a temper tantrum. We moved to adjourn. Grant extended his stay in Khartoum and we pressed ahead. Only after several more visits in which the head of the WFP, Trevor Page, joined us to press our case and Grant employed his famous charm and wits. In the end, al-Bashir complied. Lifeline was a "go" again. We began transporting thousands of tons of food up the Nile River on barges and through the savannah on the newly rehabilitated railroad, and always, by airfreight.

During this period I travelled countless junkets from outback to bush as a stowaway on cargo flights, stashed among sacks of food aid and other relief items. On such occasions, I was hard-pressed to find much glamour in my job. But on a particularly bumpy flight from Juba to Khartoum in 1988, I flew with stars in my eyes – because sitting next to me, covered in the white dust of the sacks of wheat flour that were the primary cargo contents of our flight, was Audrey Hepburn.

This was one of many instances that, had you told me would come to pass thirty years earlier, I would scarcely believe. After all, I was quite mesmerized with Audrey Hepburn and had been since she first jumped on the back of Gregory Peck's Vespa for a "Roman Holiday" in 1953. Before she became a leading lady of Hollywood, Hepburn was a hungry child in post-War Holland. When she retired from film, she turned her activities to supporting the humanitarian organization that had given her family warm clothes and medicine in the harsh years after the war. The field trip to Sudan to observe UNICEF's work was just one of many that Audrey made as a Goodwill Ambassador. She was in the late stages of her cancer at the time, and the trip presented some very physical challenges, not least of which was rising at 4 a.m. to sit on the floor of a flour-dusted Hercules cargo plane. But Audrey took all of the discomforts with the same incomparable grace that made her a movie star. To this day, when I think of all the glamorous, iconic images of this beautiful woman – as a princess, an ingénue, a debutante or muse – it is the image of her with a frail child, oblivious to the cameras around her, that most moves me.

The outcome of our multi-party negotiations was worth the blood, sweat and tears of often-rancorous talks. The ground rules we hashed out forced both sides to adhere to fundamental principals of humanitarian aid: that aid be delivered on the basis of need alone; that it be granted independent of political, race, religion, ethnicity or nationality; that passage of assistance be granted regardless of territorial occupation; that humanitarian agencies can hire their own personnel and vehicles; and that the aid agencies have a duty to ensure appropriate use of aid.

In retrospect, it is amazing that such principals are still not universally recognized and that it took such laborious negotiation to secure them. Crucially to UNICEF's credibility, the ground rule further stipulated that all parties – UNICEF, the Government of Sudan and the SPLA – were expressing support for the Geneva Conventions and the Convention on the Rights of the Child. In other words, we had won more than safe passage and promise of neutrality; we had won recognition of the fundamental standards of human rights.

Furthermore, this understanding was reached without a discussion of military enforcement. The ground rules would not require armed referees. Most significantly, the Lifeline initiative, as an operation working within a sovereign nation that recognized, on paper at least, the rights of all civilians to humanitarian assistance, established an important precedent for interventions that followed in Angola, Iraq, Somalia and Bosnia.

Drought, insecurity and poverty persisted in spite of UNICEF and its partners' progress in humanitarian priorities. By the end of the millennium, the UN was still providing a Lifeline in Sudan. In 2000 the operation totaled 24 recovery projects, run by eight UN agencies with a budget of $125 million. These programmes included food aid for close to three million people and critical services like vaccination, clean water, education and psychosocial rehabilitation for eleven million more. OLS continued for five more years, until Garang and his rebels won a stipulated autonomy. The terms for peace included scheduled elections for South Sudan in 2011. With this and many other hopeful signs of stability and normalcy, UNICEF shut down the Lifeline and celebrated its hard won success.

When in 2011, South Sudan voted for independence, it was recognized by the United Nations as the youngest independent country on the planet. Tragically, only three years later, the world's newest nation fell into internecine squabbling that escalated into violent conflict. Civil war is raging in South Sudan as I write this, and we are back to square one. Recently, the Security Council was pressed to deliver a condemnation of the hostilities, but it is a warning that falls on deaf ears. Sudan and its southern neighbor require not one, but many lifelines. The UN mission in Juba struggles to provide for tens of thousands of people fleeing the violence, sometimes within the physical confines of its bases. And if the situation is tenuous for those Sudanese, it is every bit as dangerous for the aid workers on whom they depend. Six UN workers were kidnapped in the last month alone. How can they provide a lifeline when they struggle to operate at a minimum function of protection?

Shortly after the shut-down of OLS, a Norwegian international aid worker named Svein Tore Rode-Christoffersen declared this post-mortem: "The principle is the best part of Operation Lifeline Sudan." I share Mr. Christoffersen's sentiments (as well as his name, though he is no relation to me). But I would add that the principle in question – that humanitarian aid must be prioritized above war strategies – is no small thing for warring parties to adopt, even when they fail to honor it regularly.

At the end of the day, it's not hard for me to measure the work done in Sudan with stars in my eyes. I look back at the day that Audrey Hepburn, now impeccably dressed and coiffed without a trace of the wheat flour that we had worn on our observation trip, stood before a group of big UNICEF donors to recount her impressions of Operation Lifeline. Her audience included Jim Grant and the President of the UN General Assembly. She spoke with emotion, intelligence and poise, concluding her presentation with the observation: "We have an operation that we should all be very proud of." Then she stepped to my side and hugged me, saying, "And much of it is thanks to this wonderful man and his colleagues."

I have been part of many great humanitarian endeavors, from the feeding and sheltering of displaced survivors of the killing fields on Cambodia's border to the repatriation of thousands of survivors of later genocides in central Africa. And I have travelled with, briefed, or worked with a handful of very famous people including Harry Belafonte, Peter Ustinov and Liv Ullman, whose views of the United Nations have been informed partially by my own. But never have I felt quite so high in that celestial sweet spot where good deeds and great people mingle than when I escorted Audrey Hepburn from that donor meeting.

ERITREA

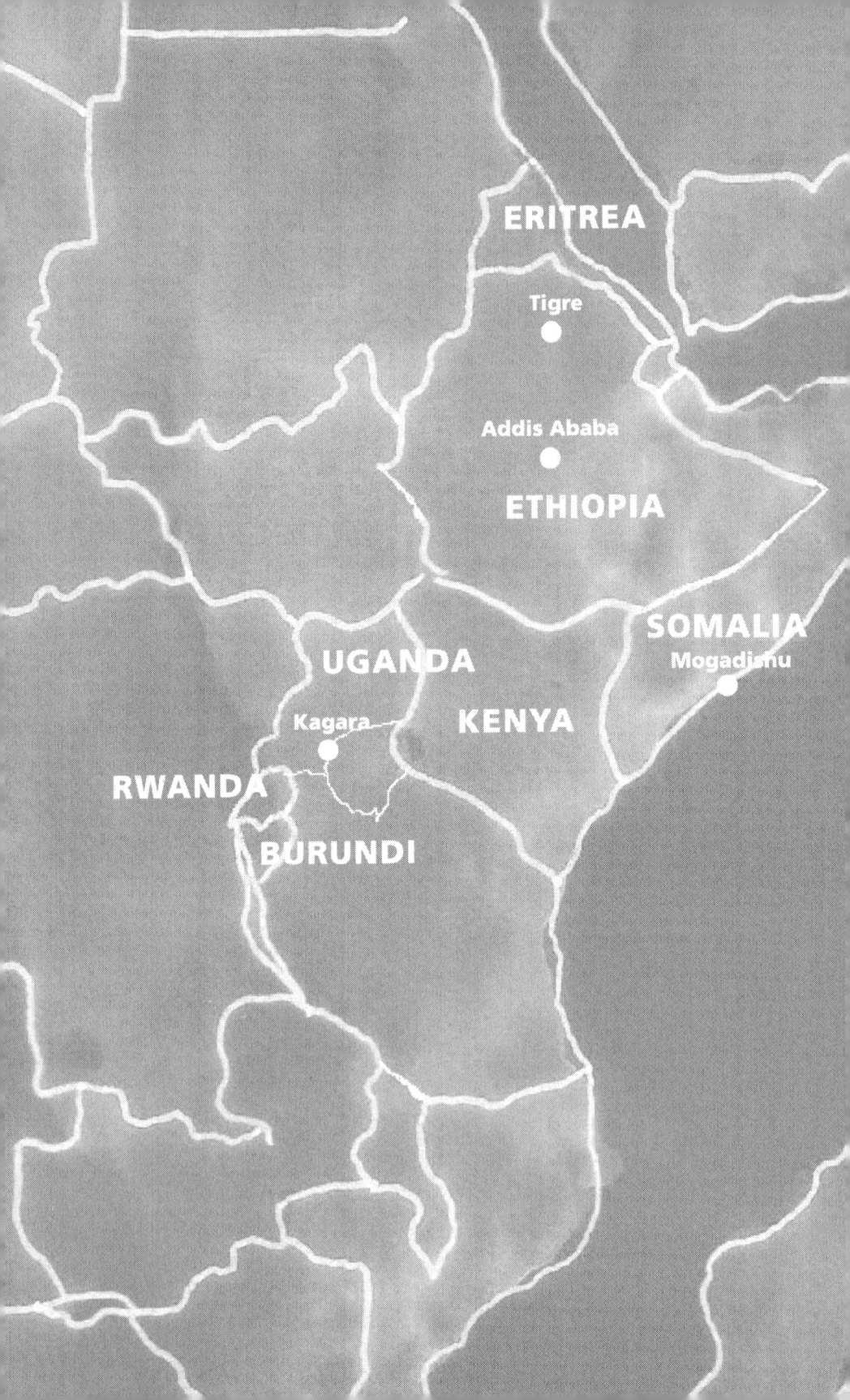

Tigre

Addis Ababa

ETHIOPIA

SOMALIA
Mogadishu

UGANDA

Kagara KENYA

RWANDA

BURUNDI

PART 4

FROM SHIELD TO TARGET

CHAPTER 16

Refugee Roots

I HAD SAILED THROUGH SEVENTEEN YEARS of service to the United Nations, weathering storms and stretches of becalmed torpor. I had crossed oceans, deserts and countless borders, relishing the physical and human landscape that differentiated one posting from another and rewarded every mission with memories. I had dined on Mediterranean fruits, West Indian delights, home-cooked Italian pasta, the fermented brews of the Masai, and once, during an infestation in Chad, pan-fried locusts. It had been, in all respects, a rich journey.

As a new decade dawned, I reviewed my career and saw a steady trajectory of accomplishment: The frustration of Phnom Penh and Laos had felt like providing assistance in straight jacket; but the accomplishment of raising a refugee camp from scratch in Aranyaprathet made those early years seem like a false start; then, accepting a wider portfolio, I had mastered effective delegation and refined diplomacy, putting me in the frontlines of Jim Grant's child survival revolution. Where would I go from here? It was a question I asked whenever I returned from a field mission to my home base at the Palais des Nations in Geneva to find a shakeup in personnel at UN's European headquarters. I had options: Should I join the Representative circuit, becoming a roving ambassador for the world's children? Should I join the upper ranks in New York and spend my next years in close rapport with the diplomats of Turtle Bay, locked in perpetual talks in the General Assembly or the ECOSOC chamber or any number of fluorescent-lit meeting rooms? Or should I aim higher with an eye on the top floors, the home of the UN Secretariat?

I think of that well-worn track even today, when I stand before the bright young men and women who fill my lecture hall at the University of Lund. "How can I work for the UN?" they ask and I explain that the UN is the United Nations – it is not singular. It is an institutional framework that, at its best, coordinates the work of an extensive network of Funds, Programmes, Councils and Agencies, and enhances their mutual work. The United Nations is about peace and humanitarian assistance, yes. But it is also about agriculture, economic development, international trade, environmental preservation and cultural heritage. Most importantly, it is a body of individuals – men and women who operate independently as often as they work together. It is they who vaccinate millions of children every year, who provide for the hundreds of thousands of refugees, and who respond to deadly disasters year after year.

Some students are interested in working in specific parts of the world, some in particular areas of development. Still others want to know the fastest, most direct way to the top, and when I hear this question - so direct and naïve - I think of my friend the Swiss policeman who cared not at all for the "United Stations." But I give them a more pragmatic answer. "Do your fieldwork," I tell them. For that is the only place you can develop the compassion, the curiosity, and most of all the grit it takes to be an effective humanitarian responder or international servant.

As for professional ambition, well there's not a thing wrong with that, either. "Always set the bar high," I once declared grandly from my lecture podium. "How high?" came a voice from the back. "Aspire to become Secretary General of the United Nations," I answered, before adding, "and know that it is the most impossible job in world."

In the last years of my tenure at UNICEF, I found myself needing a higher bar as well as more grit. I had seen with my own eyes the impact of UNICEF's emphasis on reducing child mortality: two million fewer infant deaths over ten years; soaring immunization rates worldwide; and perhaps most tellingly, the political commitment that sent seventy-one heads of state to attend the first ever World Summit on Children in 1990. But as a veteran emergency responder who had invested seventeen years in UNICEF, I had sufficient skills and experience to set off in a new direction. I was one hundred percent in favor of massive campaigns to vaccinate, hydrate, iodize and breastfeed every child on the planet, but I was ready to do more of what I do best: assist families uprooted by emergencies. So when the United Nations High Commissioner for Refugees (UNHCR) sought my services, I was happy to give them.

I was already well acquainted with UNHCR, a constant partner in UNICEF emergency operations. Founded to provide for European refugees left homeless after World War II, the agency was made a permanent institution in 1950. The following year the UN adopted the Convention on Refugees, establishing the right to asylum for anyone fleeing ethnic, religious or political persecution. While this right remains on the records, it has been eclipsed by the pressing humanitarian demands of mass migration sparked by conflict, famine and natural disaster. In the 1990's, the number of people forcibly displaced from their homes worldwide was creeping towards fifty million, a record high. A disproportionate number of these unfortunates were in Sub-Saharan Africa where the number of active conflicts spiked above fifty. Ethiopia and Sudan still bled refugees; the region of the Great Lakes seethed with ethnic conflict; and Somalia was on the brink of a major humanitarian catastrophe. I knew that my passport would once again be covered in stamps from the Horn of Africa as I tried to keep up with the revolving door of refugees.

My decision was made easier by the fact that I was on good terms with the High Commissioner herself, Sadako Ogata, who served on UNICEF's Executive Board. Impeccably coiffed and clad in Chanel, the petite Japanese diplomat wielded the strongest negotiation skills I've ever seen and could hold the attention of far more imposing physical types. She was always open to input, but if she felt strongly about an issue, no amount of advice would sway her intentions. I told myself that I had much to offer the High Commissioner, both as an emergency coordinator and as a guy who knew his way around refugee camps from Ethiopia to Cambodia.

There was another woman whose overtures I gladly accepted at this juncture as well. The second woman to win me over was a colleague, an

American woman with whom I had worked for two years in Chad. Kathleen Cravero had joined my team in 1986 and proved herself an indispensible coordinator in the time she was with us. In the time she was not with us, I began to wonder about my feelings for this dynamic, sparkling woman. She had, I admit, intrigued me the moment I met her. I had made it a rule to always meet my new staff on arrival, a lesson I learned from Paul Ignatieff, who had greeted me in Phnom Penh with a flak jacket. But never had I enjoyed this job responsibility as much as the day Kathleen Cravero crossed the tarmac to the terminal in N'Djamena, her long hair and flowing skirt suggesting a bohemian view on life. Not even Vana and Renata, the Italian nurses, could upstage that entrance.

Kathleen was young but confident, cutting her teeth on weeklong missions in the desert and winning over everyone in the office. When we caught up again a year later to reminisce about our work in Chad, I shared my feelings. We were married in 1994

But before we could streamline our careers, we had to accept another short separation – one that would find Kathleen rising in the ranks at UNICEF headquarters in New York while I dodged a few bullets halfway across the world in Somalia, a country on the brink of a refugee explosion.

CHAPTER 17

Somalia Spills Over

I F THE WORLD WAS PAYING ATTENTION to the collapse of an empire in 1991, it was the one with its seat in Moscow. In August of that year, a panel of grey-faced apparatchiks announced that the reform minded Soviet leader, Mikhail Gorbachev, had been removed from his post "due to illness." Though the coup failed in its short-term aim, it succeeded in the longer term, toppling Gorbachev along with the communist regime that both he and his hapless putchists had hoped to preserve.

As the dramatic events in Russia unfolded before a captivated global audience, a smaller upset in a country with far fewer observers was making history of its own. For if the collapse of the Soviet Union redefined the power axis at the end of the twentieth century, the overthrow of the Somali Democratic Republic provided the world with a model of a 21st century failed state. The former marked the end of a world defined by ideology; the latter cued a new battlefield in the War on Terror.

ONCE A FLOURISHING COUNTRY with a large export business, beautiful beaches and a stable military government, Somalia's plunge into anarchy was precipitous and unchecked. Almost overnight, Mogadishu was transformed from a pretty colonial-era seaside city into a hellish warren of roving armed militants. Though Somalis are relatively homogenous in terms of language, ethnicity and religion, these common traits are of lesser social importance than clan adherence. The integrity of loyalty goes deep in Somali culture, and its destructiveness is hinted at in a bleak but common saying: "Somalia and me against the world; me and my clan against Somalia; Me and my family against the clan. Me and my brother against the family. Me against my brother." In early 1991, Somalia was hurtling down this spiral of alignment.

The catalyst for Somalia's descent into "failed state" status was the overthrow of Mohamed Siad Barre, a colonial police officer turned dictator who had ruled the country since 1969. Kept in power largely by alternating support from the Soviet Union and the United States, both of which coveted Somalia as a military base and ally, Barre was left vulnerable by the end of the Cold War. A loose federation of rival clans cooperated to seize power, but without the strongman, the notion of Somalia as a unified homeland faltered. Clan warfare reigned and would continue to for two more decades. Every government that ventured to proclaim legitimacy in the midst of utter lawlessness was dead on arrival, incapable of controlling more than a sliver of the capital, Mogadishu. Warlords battled for the rest of the country.

By 2003, the fourteenth such "transitional government" was operating in exile in neighboring Kenya, threatened by the Islamic militants who adopted the failed state as an incubator for *sharia* law and jihadist training camps. Only in 2012 did the country make significant headway towards normalcy, adopting a new constitution, parliament and president for the first time in half a century.

In the decade that I worked for the High Commissioner, I would make more than a dozen trips to Somalia. I closed the UNHCR office in Mogadishu twice, reopened it twice and was evacuated twice – once in an orderly fashion and once on a wing and a prayer. But in early 1992, while in my first UNHCR position as the acting representative in Kenya, I technically had no business in Somalia. Nonetheless, that's where I was headed. The old adage about good fences is worth nothing in a refugee crisis, and Kenya's neighbor, I had determined, needed all the friends it could get.

At that time, some 400,000 refugees were living in Kenya. As Africa's most accommodating host during a decade of record-breaking refugee movements, the government of Kenya was a crucial ally for the UNHCR. Nairobi willingly opened its borders to refugees not just from Somalia, but from every country on its perimeter, each of which was experiencing conflict and food insecurity. But if the government's hospitality knew no limits, its physical territory did. While some of the Somali refugees managed to integrate into the urban populations in Mombasa or Nairobi, the vast majority was confined to residence in six official camps. The camps in Kenya were paragons of safe, serviced, secure asylum. Indeed, they provided so many basic services and comforts that, in time, our problem became how to encourage repatriation.

This catch-22 of providing reliable food, water, shelter and medical care in a part of the world where none of those things are taken for granted became evident to me some years ago when a young man who was taking my course on international development at the University of Lund in Sweden approached me to say that he had been born and raised in one of the Kenyan refugee camps that I helped set up in the early 1990s. He recalled a spartan but secure childhood, filled with an abundance of neighbors and playmates.

I knew from my experience in Cambodia the vast gap between a protective camp and a dangerous one. The first line of defense, and the one that UNHCR and UNCEF both have had heroic roles in creating, is in the basic sanitary structures and vaccination regimes to prevent epidemics and outbreaks of waterborne diseases.

There is far less that aid workers can do for women and children in these camps to provide basic security against unsavory elements who abuse the refuge. Every camp I have ever known attracts a criminal element. It is the job of the host country, and not the UNHCR, to guard against their unwanted presence on a daily basis and protect aid workers from the risk they present at night. But in the absence of peacekeepers (and the only refugee camp I have ever known that was guarded by peacekeepers was in Darfur), such protection is not always satisfactorily accomplished.

It is not the aid workers who suffer from this lack of security; it is the women and girls. There is nothing more outrageous than the disproportionate violence directed at women in conflict zones everywhere, where rape is a weapon of war. This appalling weapon does not excuse itself from the refugee camps, where women bear the brunt of the labor, fetching water and firewood far from the security of their tents. They are all too often victimized as they do.

That we could not, and cannot, always protect these women as emergency aid workers remains a vexing point. It is easy to argue that having a nighttime presence in the camps could reduce the rate of attacks. The problem with this scenario is that the UN's responsibility to its own workers would necessitate a resource-draining contingent of personal security for workers actually living in the camps. And why should we be protected while the women most in need of protection are not? There are enough double standards in the distribution of aid without our necessitating more.

In the case of the Somalian refugee explosion, Kenya was doing an excellent job absorbing asylum seekers at considerable expense. The presence of a large foreign community takes an environmental toll, creates social tensions with host communities, and presents a threat to national security, particularly if the refugees are fleeing civil unrest that might follow them across borders. I did not want to see a situation that would make the government in Nairobi regret its open-door policy.

A visit to Mandera, a town tucked into the triangle between the borders of Ethiopia, Somalia and Kenya, convinced me of the urgency of stemming the flow. An unforeseen uprising across the border in Bulo Hawa, Somalia had sent 10,000 refugees spilling into central Mandera, a town ill equipped to shelter this sudden influx. One look at the saturated town square was enough to convince me to broker an arrangement with the leaders of the Somali group that had incited the violence. I told my driver and the colleague accompanying me that we were going further east, across the border to Bulo Hawa.

When we arrived, I drew upon my well-learned lesson as a peacekeeper to always demonstrate esteem for the local leaders. Over a full day of respectful dialogue I implored the elders to show munificence and protection for their countrymen, some of whom may or not be clan members. I got what I had come for: an agreement to welcome back the Somalis who had fled to Mandera. The elders agreed to assist, and I promised the UNHCR's support in return. Pleased with the success of my unauthorized visit, I climbed back into our vehicle to return to Kenya.

Halfway to the border we were stopped by eight men. Their tight grips on their weapons told me they were in charge of the situation. Their agitated eyes, showing the tell-tale signs of qat, the natural narcotic used by fighters across the Horn, told me this was an unfortunate turn of events. The leader of the group had clearly been maimed by an explosive, and his lack of a lower jaw gave him an especially diabolical air. He harangued his rag-tag team and I understood nothing. Then he turned to me with perfectly intelligible demands: He wanted our vehicle, the contents of the vehicle, and all our money. I played my citizen of the world card, explaining that I was a UN official returning from a mission that would be beneficial to his people. The jawless man just looked at me. His eyes had gone as vacant as his lower face. I knew we had been indefinitely waylaid.

My next move was to drop the name of a powerful tribal leader with whom I had already spoken in Mandera. He may have been a refugee in Kenya, but his guarantee of free passage across the border was as reliable as any official document in these lawless parts. I told the jumpy gunman to send one of his men to Mandera and to ask Mohammed Ali to vouch for our presence. Even today the entreaty amuses me: "Ask Mohammed Ali. He'll back me up."

By nightfall, the jawless man's envoy had still not returned. Fatigued, hungry, thirsty and not a little uneasy, my colleagues and I hunkered down by the car to sleep. I passed a restless night thinking about the repercussions should this mission go belly-up. I tried not to think about the fact that the only person on the planet who knew more or less where to find us was Mohammed Ali, the refugee. I tried, not very successfully, to believe that I would return to Kenya alive.

The next day was agonizingly hot. With no shade and with lingering optimism, I passed the day cursing my impulsive mission. Finally the envoy returned with confirmation. Mohammed Ali had come through, and we were free to go —just as soon as his gang had stripped us of everything including the Land Cruiser's spare tire. As we drove away from our twenty-four hour-long hostage ordeal, I half expected a bullet in the back. We drove through the night and arrived back at Kakuma camp in the morning.

I didn't report the incident to the High Commissioner or to my superiors until some time later, when I was back in Geneva. By then, the trauma of the hostage event had dissipated. All that was left was the satisfaction of having provided an alternative to an untenable situation in Mandera.

In retrospect, this achievement strikes me as both important and, ultimately negligible. Within weeks of our brokered repatriation, violence broke out again in Bula Howa. Mandera was again full of refugees. This time we acknowledged the pointlessness of sending them that back into conflict. However the Kenyan government was not comfortable allocating land so near the border with both Somalia and Ethiopia. There was no alternative but to move the refugees further into Kenya and into already established camps like Libor and Kakuma.

Though UNHCR and the Kenyan Government have continued to strive to keep populations manageable, sometimes resorting to these massive relocations, conditions for the entrenched refugees are not impeccable. Kakuma, still home to 55,000 refugees today, has been the site of multiple disease outbreaks including cholera and malaria. Crime is another epidemic in Kakuma today – another painful acknowledgement that no humanitarian provision can fully counterbalance the inherent instability of an impoverished, stateless, hopeless population with limited options.

As one of the world's chief humanitarian agencies, UNHCR aids millions of displaced people every year in more than 100 countries. It relies on a yearly budget of $1 billion to do so – less if the government member states do not pay their full dues, which does happen. The men and women who work to provide for the hundreds of thousands of refugees in Africa's Horn, a population that grows every year, are not social workers. They are not ministers or counselors or therapists. They are not trained to handle individual needs, only human needs. Like the Blue Berets of the early UN, they are trained to *defuse* not to *prevent*. Their job is to mitigate hunger, disease, vulnerability and exploitation, but not to eradicate it.

If the camps for Somali refugees presented a certain level of danger for UN and NGO workers, it was of the sort that has been the reality of aid work since the beginning of time: insecurity. Crowds are dangerous; hungry crowds more so; and desperate crowds naturally so. A refugee camp brings crowds, darkness, close quarters and mixed loyalties together.

"You cannot create an island of security in a sea of insecurity," a colleague once said to me, and I cannot argue with that. Even my experience as a peacekeeper, during a period when the flag-flying white UN vehicle was imagined as a mobile island of security, had led me to understand deeply the shortcomings.

By the 1990s eastern Africa and the Horn was plagued with armed struggle, genocidal conflict and Islamic fundamentalism. These impediments make aid work virtually impossible without peacekeeping. In some places, those troops were provided either as UN forces or through the accords with regional alliances like the AEU or ECOWAS. But they, too, were subject to the risks of a theatre with far too many armed players. I had to conclude that not only was the UN logo no shield … it had become a target.

CHAPTER 18

The Pain of Mogadishu

IF I HAD ANY ILLUSIONS about the sanctity of the UN shield, they were put to rest in June 1993 when I twice found myself a decidedly persona-non-grata in the Somali capital, Mogadishu.

By then, the United States had raised its response to the lawlessness in Somalia and sent marines to secure the port and airfield for a humanitarian airlift of supplies. Meanwhile, at the UN, Secretary General Boutros Boutros Ghali asked the Security Council to authorize peacekeepers throughout the country. Equally promising, some fifteen separate Somali factions attended peace talks in Addis Ababa and found common ground on an unprecedented number of terms. For a time, all was going according to the best-laid UN scenarios: There was an international coalition of support, there was a humanitarian effort, and there was progress on internal reconciliation. And then came Aidid.

Mohamed Farrah Aidid was just one of a dozen warlords with a dog in the fight for Somalia. He was part of the rebel force that drove out Siad Barre, but he had not found much traction during the infighting that followed. Until, that is, the UN made its presence felt in Somalia. Beginning with rancorous radio broadcasts, Aidid challenged the US and the UN as occupiers plotting Somalia's demise. The antagonism became fatal on June 5, when Aidid's forces attacked a brigade of Pakistani peacekeepers, killing twenty-four and wounding dozens more. Secretary Boutros-Ghali denounced the attack, and the Security Council passed a resolution calling for Aidid's prosecution. It was the closest the UN had ever come to declaring war and an outright reversal of the Charter's provision of political neutrality. All UN agencies, including the UNHCR office, were closed and staffs evacuated.

By October, the US had committed to full combat to remove Aidid from the scene. The trouble was finding him. The warlord had gone to ground, but American intelligence had located two of his deputies, and when the intelligence was confirmed a special ops force was tasked with extracting them. The operation by Task Force Ranger was supposed to last thirty minutes. It went terribly wrong. The Pentagon had misjudged the local population as well as the capabilities of Aidid's forces, which managed to shoot down the two Black Hawk helicopters and ensnare the special ops team in a tense overnight standoff as they tried to recover their downed comrades. Twelve hours and an intense firefight later, eighteen marines were dead. The United States, humiliated and shocked by the spectacle of its mutilated marines paraded through the streets of Mogadishu, withdrew from Somalia entirely. The battle would live in infamy as the Black Hawk Down disaster. The side of the story that is less often told is that scores of Somalis died that day as well. They believed they were defending their homes. Many of them – women and children used as human shields – in fact, were.

Ten months after the battle of Mogadishu, I returned to the war-torn city to close up the office and retrieve all of our valuable satellite equipment. When the job was done and all the documents shredded, I was advised to travel to an airstrip in the northern part of the city. This was the only airstrip that was not in the hands of Aidid's forces, and a Red Cross plane was scheduled to ferry a handful of NGO stragglers out of the city. We had just left the office when my driver and I found ourselves caught in crossfire. We jumped out of the car and took cover under the chassis. At the first lull in the shooting, we were back in the car; This time I was behind the wheel. Following my driver's navigation I tore through the city to reach the airstrip. We didn't make it. The ambush had delayed us over an hour and the Red Cross plane did not wait. I sent the driver back to the city to contact the Red Cross representative and to plead for a second flight on my behalf. Then I hunkered down to wait, alone, in perhaps the only quiet corner of Mogadishu.

As I sat in the spookily quiet terminal, praying for a miracle, I heard the whine of an engine overhead. Rushing to the tarmac, I saw a wreck of a two-engine craft descend shakily in the heat. This was no Red Cross plane, I realized, as a dozen men emerged from the bushes to greet it. I paused for a moment, watching this pit crew quickly unload bundles from the cargo hold. Then I approached the pilot, a Kenyan who agreed to give me a lift for $200. I paid up, not even bothering to ask where he was headed. Only when we were airborne did I realize that I was escaping Mogadishu in a drug-smuggler's plane. I spent the trip laughing hysterically at the image of me pushing bundles of qat through the rusted-out holes in the floor – a perverse sort of humanitarian airdrop.

When we landed at Winston airport in Nairobi, I invented all sorts of tales for the customs officer to keep my qat smuggler savior out of trouble. Then I called a colleague and asked him to pick me up and take me to the nearest cold bottle of Tusker lager.

My adventures in Mogadishu were not over, however. In early 1994, the Security Council revised the peacekeeping mandate for Somalia to emphasize reconciliation. Some fifteen political parties in Mogadishu got on board as well, agreeing to a ceasefire, disarmament and a conference to appoint a new government. That was UNHCR's cue to put out the welcome mat once more. Madame Ogata ordered me back to the capital to prepare for the repatriation of the thousands of citizens of Mogadishu who had been sitting out the violence in neighboring refugee camps. It was a decision more political than practical, since it was far from certain that this future appointed government in place would actually manage to govern once in place.

Because re-opening an office is the equivalent of re-opening an embassy in a sovereign state, the duty was mine. I asked my old comrade Vincent O'Reilly, who was running UNICEF's Somali operations out of Kenya, to accompany me. He agreed - a decision he would later regret as our exit from the city proved even more terrifying than my escape with the qat smuggler. We had a security detail, though we felt none too secure in their company. They were the best Mogadishu had to offer in body men: young, industrious, and in possession of a hijacked truck and plenty of firepower. These "technicals" were abundant in the city and their services were obligatory for all international entities – if for no other reason than the fact that if you did not employ them, they would likely shoot you themselves.

The tension in the city was high and we found ourselves the object of agitation everywhere we went. Our "technicals" navigated us from one dicey situation to the next all the way to the airport gate. It was here, steps away from our exit, that we found ourselves completely surrounded by agitated, qat–chewing, militants. The more aggressive of the gun-toters began to rock our car and insist that we leave or be shot. O'Reilly hit the floor and started invoking every Catholic saint in the book. I pointed demonstratively at the plane a hundred yards in the distance that I promised would assist me in leaving if the men who so wanted us gone would just allow us egress. My negotiations grew more panicked as I saw the propellers begin to turn. I was really not prepared to wait for another miracle second-chance flight out of Mogadishu. Just then our dubious protector, the head of our "technical," adorned with Ray Bans and a bandolier of ammo, made himself heard loud and clear. I have no idea what he said to convince the angry mob to let us go. It may have been punctuated with bullets in the air; I don't recall. But minutes later we were on that plane. Vincent continued to thank the saints throughout the whole flight. But he didn't express any gratitude to me.

I observed Mogadishu from many vantages in the early 1990s. I saw its innocent population trapped in a hellish firefight, but I also saw the distrust that radiated from those innocents – and it was often directed at me. I eyed the city from street-level, never sure that harm did not stalk me from around the next corner; But I also saw it through the hole between my legs in a rusted out smuggling plane. No matter where I was in that city – in a car, plane, office or under guard, I was intensely aware of my lack of security. It was a sensation that I became used to. After all, no one in the city was safe. But the palpable peril raised in me a familiar skepticism about the ultimate duty of the United Nations to protect its own. Mogadishu has come a long way since the terror and anarchy of 1992, but the insecurity is ratcheting up again. Today, in addition to militants and criminals, aid workers are confronted with the terrorism of the Al-Shabab. In June 2013, assailants attacked the UN compound and killed eight UN employees and several Somali civilians. None of them were soldiers; the blue flag flying above the compound was provocation enough.

CHAPTER 19

Rwanda, Failure to Protect

I WAS IN GENEVA, preparing to take up a position as the UNHCR Representative in Uganda, when I read Romeo Dallaire's alarming memorandum from Kigali in January 1994. The Rwandan Hutu government, he warned, planned to force the removal of UN peacekeepers from the country in order to effect an "anti-Tutsi extermination." This was the first in a series of increasingly urgent dispatches from Dallaire, the Canadian commander of the peacekeeping operation in Kigali, to the head of DPKO and the UN Secretariat in New York. Later communications would plead for reinforcements and for armed intervention. But Dallaire's warnings and entreaties failed to prevent the 100-day massacre that we now call the Rwandan genocide.

Dallaire's intelligence was correct. Extremists in the political elite, ethnic Hutus, were plotting to wipe out the minority Tutsi population. In April, the plane carrying the President, a Hutu, was shot down and the moderates in his government were assassinated. And, just as Dallaire had warned, the UN was targeted: ten peacekeepers, Belgian Blue Helmets assigned to guard the Prime Minister, were captured, tortured and murdered. This was less than one year after the murder of Pakistani peacekeepers in Mogadishu. But in contrast to the UN response to those deaths - a virtual declaration of war against Farrah Aidid - the Security Council responded to the brazen killing in Kigali by voting unanimously to withdraw nearly all of the 2,500 peacekeepers in the country. Commander Dallaire was left with just a few hundred soldiers – Canadians, Ghanaians, Tunisians and Bangladeshis. They watched helplessly as, over the next three months, 800,000 ethnic Tutsis were slaughtered by former friends and neighbors. Twenty years after the genocide, observers are still trying to explain the mass psychosis that allowed such an atrocity to take place and the global temerity that allowed it to go unchecked.

The failure of the UN to prevent the Rwandan genocide is, on its face, inexcusable. And yet ... there are excuses; simple explanations that are frustrating, even infuriating in their correctness. The first has to do with resources: Rwanda was one of twenty-eight conflicts that the United Nations was committed to resolving in 1994. The ill-fated peacekeeping force that Lieutenant-General Dallaire commanded was one of seventeen such operations. That represented a tripling in commitments over seven years earlier, but at fifteen times the cost. Stretched thin and across conflicts that required far more boots on the ground to enforce a peace that had not yet been established, the Department of Peacekeeping Operations was underfunded and overcommitted.

The second weakness at this juncture was the UN charter that made policing internal conflicts so much more politically challenged than multi-state conflicts. Because the founding states were wary of unwanted meddling in sovereign affairs, to this day the UN is only able to intervene at the invitation of a member state and resolution of the fifteen-member Security Council. This precaution has become a trap that ensnares good-intentioned missions to prevent bloodshed everywhere. The neutrality of the United Nations is forever compromised by the fact that the executor of the UN's peacemaking bodies, the Security Council, is made up of non-neutral members.

The most appalling instance of this legality today is in Syria, where the UN has no hope of sending referees and struggles mightily to gain access for humanitarian relief. This is because Syria's representative, bolstered by the presence of its ally Russia in a permanent seat of the Security Council, has blocked all resolutions to commit aid. As a result, the civil war has lasted four long years and taken more than 150,000 innocent victims. Even this impediment pales in comparison to the 800,000 deliberate deaths in Rwanda over 100 days in 1994. The blame for the massacre often falls on France, which as the historical ally of the Hutu government used its Security Council vote to stall a response. In truth, the United States, burned by its intervention in Mogadishu, was equally indecisive.

As gruesome as those one hundred days were for witnesses in Rwanda (Dallaire left the experience severely damaged, speaking out publically about the suicidal symptoms of PTSD), they were nearly as unbearable for those of us who watched the United Nations stab itself in the back over and over again. The genocide is a traumatic memory for any international civil servant or diplomat; not least of all for Kofi Annan, who, as head of DPKO during the genocide, toed the chain of command. It was Annan who brought Dallaire's request for an infusion of soldiers to the Security Council. It was Annan who reported to Dallaire that his request could not be fulfilled, blocked by a veto by France. It was Annan who, years later, as Secretary General, visited the Great Lakes Region and made a personal apology to the Rwandan refugees who had survived the genocide.

I was present for that event, and though he may not have won over his audience, the new SG gained my respect that day. Because I knew perfectly well that Kofi Annan was not solely to blame; no more than the slain Belgian peacekeepers were the sole victims of the Security Council stalemate. I thought it grossly unfair that Annan was blamed for acting on instructions from his superiors.

During the Rwanda crisis, the United States deflected responsibility. Still smarting from the "Black Hawk Down" debacle in Mogadishu, President Bill Clinton and his national security team were timorous of foreign intervention in a bloody ethnic conflict. Instead, the US government washed its hands of "other people's problems." Without the leadership of Washington, the UN proved equally impotent in stopping the genocide. It was a nadir for the organization's peacekeeping department and for the Security Council, where circumspection and politics won the day.

That said, Rwanda also marked an important sea change in the UN's decades-long policy of deferring to sovereign invitations. The calamitous results of the international community's neglect were too shocking to ignore. The genocide prompted real soul searching and a concerted drive to institute policies that would prevent another such failure. Kofi Annan, the man who as head of DPKO during Rwanda's upheaval had born a massive burden of impotence and remorse, ushered in the new millennium with an important new vision for the organization. As Secretary General, Annan spoke of "gross and systematic violations of human rights [that] offends every precept of our common humanity." Annan called on the international community to find a consensus on new parameters for humanitarian intervention beyond peacekeeping and into protection. From this debate came a new norm known as Responsibility to Protect, or R2P.

Today R2P is still being tested – in Eastern Congo, in Central African Republic, in South Sudan and in Syria. These are conflicts that test the commitment of the international community on a near daily basis. Many of them are intractable – entering into their second or third wave of violence excited by shifting alliances and militant groups. Many of them are chronic largely because of political stalemates between the indirectly involved players in the Security Council. When Russia vetoes a resolution on Syria, or France negotiates intervention in Mali, or the United States brings false testimony to the General Assembly, the purity of R2P as a principal is hijacked. Today, R2P, awe-inspiring on paper and stalking the globe, is little more than a paper tiger. Until it shows its claws, we cannot judge its power.

PERSONALLY, WHENEVER I FIND MYSELF TIED UP in knots trying to explain or justify the UN's inaction in Rwanda, I think back to the first week of my post as the UNHCR Representative in Uganda. I travelled straight from the capital to a refugee camp on the banks of Lake Victoria where thousands of Tutsi survivors, the lucky ones who escaped the murderous mass psychosis of their countrymen, had sheltered. They were in grave need of psychosocial support, and many required medical attention. But I did not immediately concern myself with camp matters or with protocol. My first task was to join the other volunteers from the UN and NGO community in collecting the bloated bodies floating down the Kagera River from Rwanda before they could accumulate on the shores of the refugee camp. We knew that sparing the survivors this last trauma was the least we could do.

CHAPTER 20
Uganda, Aftermath of Genocide

I WAS A MARRIED MAN IN KAMPALA, one half of a modestly historic couple – the first ever concurrent, married representatives of two UN agencies in a single country. Kathleen and I had to do a lot of talking to overcome the reservations about this unorthodox appointment, but we never regretted it.

Uganda was a major field of operations for the High Commissioner of Refugees in the 1990's. Much in the way Kenya was absorbing refugees from all quarters, Uganda was the preferred asylum for refugees from Congo, Rwanda and, shortly after my arrival, South Sudan, which was undergoing another paroxysm of violence.

In contrast to the predicament in Kenya, where refugees were steadily turning their temporary asylum into permanent residence, the camps in northern Uganda were a veritable revolving door. An influx of refugees – whole villages in exodus – would be followed by a repatriation of another community. It took an economic and sociopolitical toll on the government, this ongoing human churn. So in this instance, I saw the benefits that could come to these people by establishing a more permanent settlement, or at least a settlement that could provide some normalcy rather than a temporary solution. Though the red flags of permanence were waving, we had to consider every situation on its own merits. And in this scenario, a longer-term accommodation made sense for the refugees and also for the Ugandan government. I had the support and regular cooperation of the Interior Minister, a man named Mr. Carlos, who accompanied me regularly to the site.

But first I had to clear the scheme with the big boss – President Yoweri Museveni. I got my chance on a Sunday morning when the phone rang and an unidentified man announced that the president wished to speak with me. It took me half a minute to understand: *Why would the President of Uganda call me at 7 a.m. on a Sunday?* I got the answer quickly: "Kristoffersson? I want to see you. I want to hear your ideas on my refugees."

I pondered this request as I hurriedly shaved and dressed. "My refugees," he had said. A good sign. When I arrived at the President's residence I was received immediately, another good sign and a rare event in my previous experiences with Heads of State.

We found a shared language that day, President Museveni and I. In fact we found more than one common tongue. I had imagined that as a war hero, former rebel commander who had fought guerilla wars in Mozambique and against the despotic Idi Amin, Museveni would be impressed with my military discipline. But when I told him about my Marine training he just exclaimed, "Sweden! Sweden gave my family sanctuary." As it turned out, the President had real sympathy with the plight of the refugee. His wife and children had been given asylum in my home country during his campaign against Amin.

A few days later, the Minister of the Interior and I traveled to the district of Arua to scout possible territory for a settlement. Within weeks we were building proper infrastructure: roads, irrigation, health centers, and schools. Determined to make the settlement a viable harmonious community, assimilated and self-sufficient, I insisted that the infrastructure we were providing be sufficient for both refugees and the local Ugandan community. This was critical to maintaining good relations between the Ugandans and the transient visitors whom they already resented. This was a dynamic that could be found all over Africa, ground zero for so much displacement. Nearly one-third of all African refugees settle most immediately in a country that is itself embroiled in, or just recuperating from armed conflict as well.

It's a sobering thought – being so desperate as to flee to Ethiopia under Mengistu or to Bashir's Sudan. But imagine that you are the embattled, struggling survivors of hardship in your own homeland and that you must watch convoys of humanitarian aid lumber past for delivery up the road to foreign visitors. I was very cognizant of this fragile nuance. I was equally concerned about the environmental fragility of the land we were appropriating. Camps, whether temporary or permanent, take a toll on the land. Construction erodes the soil, and sanitation facilities must be correctly planned to ensure that the ground water is not contaminated.

The ease with which Museveni accepted these people and worked with me to make their integration in Uganda possible was characteristic of the leader whom so many western diplomats and politicians praised as a prototype of a "new African generation." The world had high hopes for Museveni in the mid-1990s. He had helped end a brutal regime and civil war and ushered in growth and stability. He had committed himself to ending corruption, sectarian violence and, most commendably for an African leader, HIV/AIDS. I was among his fans, won over by his straightforwardness and charisma. I believed Museveni was a brave pioneer – and not just in treatment of refugees. The plague of HIV was taking a terrible toll on the country: entire villages laid waste and hundreds of thousands of children orphaned. Despite its ubiquity, the disease was a taboo subject and a social stigma. Museveni was one of very few African leaders who not only discussed the virus, but also took measures to fight it by promoting abstinence, monogamy and condoms.

Sadly, my hero's democratic and human rights record has been seriously compromised. But if Museveni's disregard for democratic freedoms is universally abhorred, the authoritarian tactics of his protégé, the Rwandan President Paul Kagame, are more controversial. Kagame was the 36-year-old head of the Tutsi Rwandan Political Front that routed the Hutu government genocidaires in July 1994. Though educated and trained in the west and militarily and financially backed by Museveni, Kagame was no one's pawn. From the moment he became the de facto leader, Kagame was in complete control of the violated nation, which elected him President in 2003. Since then, Kagame, like Museveni, has discarded the trappings of western-style democracies – term limits, opposition parties and a free press among them – for more authoritarian governance. There is growing concern over his authoritarian methods and his contempt for detractors.

But Kagame has much to show for his tight fist: He has enforced a non-punitive national reconciliation, amnestying tens of thousands of convicted war criminals in the name of ethnic harmony; he has overseen an emotionally and politically fraught process of peaceful resettlement; and, if that were not ambitious enough, he has established Rwanda as a beacon of good governance, economic health, social stability and security. These achievements, miraculous in and of themselves, are particularly extraordinary given that they have been reached in just two decades. But in the months after the bloodletting, Kagame's first order of business was to bring his people home.

Close to 100,000 Tutsis who survived the massacre in Rwanda were sheltering in Uganda. The vast majority of them were housed in the Mbarara camp near Lake Victoria. They had been there for eighteen months when one morning in late 1995, I received a bewildered call from the camp's field officer.

"They're gone," he said.

"What do you mean, they're gone?" I asked.

"Come see for yourself."

When I arrived at the camp some hours later, I was greeted with an eerie spectacle. Where once 89,000 people had tended their fires, their children, and their cattle across twenty-five square acres of land, there was now nothing to break the silence. I had seen this in Cambodia – large flows out of the camp and back into the country, a collective response to a faceless summons to retake their homes and villages. But never had I seen a camp empty itself so entirely and so quickly. Here in Mbarara, there was no question as to who was behind the mass exit. As I picked my way through the ghost-camp, a barren plain marked only with the odd discarded item – an unrepaired cooking pot or a child's left shoe – I could almost hear Kagame's directive, passed word-of-mouth along the bloody road from Kigali across the deserted frontier: *Come back. Come back and help me ensure that we will overcome.*

Would that all repatriations went as smoothly and peacefully as that of the Rwandan refugees from Uganda. But they did not, and they do not.

Broadly speaking, there are three gradations in the group dynamics of refugee populations. There are refugees who are ready to return home at any cost, physical, financial or psychological. Sometimes, this return is premature and ends in tragedy. Then there are those like the Rwandans who wait for the all-clear signal and then and only then, pack for home. And then there is a third group – those who size up the benefits of refugee status and resolve to leverage them as long as possible.

Those were the refugees I had to contend with in my next assignment as the High Commissioner's representative in Burundi.

CHAPTER 21

Burundi, Point Blank

BURUNDI, A MAGNIFICENTLY BEAUTIFUL COUNTRY of lush mountain valleys, was burdened with the same ethnic tension that tore apart its northern neighbor, Rwanda. Bloodshed and indiscriminate violence between the Hutu and Tutsi groups was a near constant in the years after the country's independence. Twice, the country was racked by genocidal seizures: In 1972, Tutsis slaughtered Hutus, and in 1993, Hutus slaughtered Tutsis. The latter - a massacre of some 25,000 people - was upstaged by Rwanda's larger bloodbath and was characterized as genocide only in the final report of an International Commission. Easier to declare was that Burundi was having a civil war.

Despite the ongoing tension, in April 1996, I was dispatched to the country to prepare for the imminent return of 350,000 Burundians who had fled their homeland over the past five years. They were mostly Hutus, fearing reprisals for what their ethnic kinsmen had done to Tutsis. Assured by the progress of peace talks in Tanzania that it was safe to come back, hundreds of thousands of them were now amassing on all of Burundi's borders. UNHCR was tasked with setting up and securing transit camps where the returnees could be supplied with seed, clothing and basic necessary home supplies as they awaited settlement.

When Kathleen and I took up our posts, there was a brand new government in place in Bujumbura – one recognized by the United Nations, if not by the African nor European Unions. President Pierre Buyoya, a Tutsi, had seized power in a coup d'état. Branded by the west and by its neighbors as a rogue regime, Burundi was slapped with sanctions and boycotts. The UN, on the other hand, had sent a Special Envoy to attempt to find conciliation where others could not.

I was on the last Sabena Belgian Airline flight into the country. Kathleen was two months behind me, finishing out her UNICEF contract in Uganda. When her term was up, she travelled overland via Kigali. I drove up to the Rwanda/Burundi border to meet her and our Alsatian Shepherd, Daim. We hadn't made much progress on the road back to the capital when our convoy came under fire. The car in front of ours was hit. Kathleen, Daim and I scrambled out of our vehicle and took cover on the side of the road. We stayed there for hours, waiting for the shooting to end. Daim, I would say, was the calmest of the three of us. This was our first audience with the so-called "musique des montagnes," the "music of the mountains" that accompanied daily life in Bujumbora. We never did develop a taste for it.

The schizophrenic nature of life in Bujumbura took a heavy toll on my psyche. We lived in a beautiful house at the top of a beautiful hill overlooking what should have been objectively, a beautiful city. But we were never at ease. We had round-the-clock security, and twenty-four-hour anxiety. In the capital, the tensions were unspoken, but easily read. One morning I awoke in a sweat, sensing that something was terribly wrong. It took me a few minutes to understand what it was that I was tuning into – the quiet. It was a weekday and yet the street outside our residence, which on any other morning would be filled with the largely Hutu working-class trudging down to the homes of the wealthy Tutsi and expatriate community to clean, drive or care for the children. But on this morning some message had been passed through the city that I was not privy to, but which I could easily decode by the emptiness of that street. In Bujumbura, guerillas could attack on a moment's notice and hold the city under temporary siege before being repulsed back into the hills. This was one of those days. I knew because of the absence of day-workers: It was not a good day to go to work.

There were many days when I, too, felt little compulsion to go to work. The combination of loud violence and quiet menace was eroding my confidence and even my enthusiasm for the work I had always loved. I recall confiding to a colleague whom I knew from my UNICEF days the idea that I might be "washed up" and done with the life of an emergency responder and hardship humanitarian. We were sitting on the beautiful terrace, sipping wine and talking. And yet I could not enjoy the beauty. Too oppressive was the sense that our work was never done – that there were endless victims in the world and that their defenders would become victims too. My colleague, Pierce Garrity, didn't judge me for my uncertainty. Indeed, he nodded and confessed that at age fifty-something, he was feeling the same way. We drank in silence, taking in the view and the sounds of distant bombardments. Two weeks later I learned that Pierce had died in an airplane crash over Canada.

In addition to the native Burundians whom UNHCR was tasked with repatriating, there were hundreds of thousands of refugees from neighboring countries creating challenges within Burundi. The larger Great Lakes region was a veritable whirlpool of displacement at that time. No other spot in the world saw as much human churn in the 1990s as the countries of Rwanda, Burundi, Uganda, Tanzania and Congo, which seemed to be trading refugee populations from one month to the next in tandem with shifting political allegiances in all these states. Burundi, despite its own domestic unrest and political isolation, was hosting refugees from Rwanda and Congo – two nations with multiple ethnic groups to their name.

Though there were two camps in Burundi designated specifically for the estimated 27,000 people from the Democratic Republic of Congo, there was also a cohort of young men who had ensconced themselves in the capital as self-proclaimed urban refugees with rights to the High Commissioner's most generous aid. These men, who travelled freely between Congo and Burundi and engaged in black market trade of foreign aid, were of the third type of refugee – those that can, but won't, go home.

The world is full of migrants who correctly assess their host country a better place to live than their homeland. Unlike the vast majority of émigrés who work hard to build a new life in their new home, the Congolese thugs of Bujumbura were quite simply abusing the assistance of the international community and the generosity of their hosts. They had been milking the system quite effectively for some years under my predecessor when I decided to call their bluff. I gathered the dozen lead abusers and let them know that the "urban refugee programme" was out of funds. They should either find work to support themselves, return to Congo permanently, or join the camp population by year-end.

I knew, of course, that this news was not going to go down very well, but I was taken aback at the virulence of the response. The death threats began immediately. I had made the UN some fresh enemies. The aggression of these men, deprived of the humanitarian assistance that I planned to redistribute to women and children in real need, became a permanent condition of our posting in Burundi. Ironically ... their persistence would also save my life.

Ethnic tensions were being stoked all over the country by way of the Buyoya government's "regroupment" policy. Claiming that the Hutu populations were vulnerable to Tutsi extremists that the government could not control, Buyoya's army had taken to herding civilians into "protection sites" that lacked adequate basic shelter, food, water and sanitation. These were not UNHCR camps, but we had no option but to demand a role in order to redress the common grievance heard from the regrouped that "we live in misery so that people in the capital can live in security." The few independent observations of these camps indicated that they were rife with human rights abuses: involuntary detention, arbitrary restrictions, not to mention rape, violence and child recruitment.

In October 1999, the country team led by Kathleen, as Resident Coordinator of all UN agencies in Burundi, organized a high-level delegation to inspect one of these "regroupment" sites in the southern province of Rutana. She informed the government that we would be taking this fact-finding mission the next day

On the morning of our mission to Rutana, fate and the intransigent Congolese intervened. Just before Kathleen and I were to depart for the airport, I got a call from the office. The angry disavowed "urban refugees" had stormed the office and threatened to blow it up with a hand grenade if I did not appear and hear their demands. Kathleen and I agreed that I needed to stay behind.

It was a chaotic scene in the office and a repeat tragicomedy of negotiation, but the details of that particular repartee escape me. They are overshadowed by what happened in Rutana when my colleagues arrived to inspect the camp. They had just reached the perimeter when they were ambushed by gunmen who shot and killed two of our party. I learned this news from another colleague, who was passing it on third hand. The messenger, a staffer at the World Food Programme, probably didn't even realize the psychic damage he was doing when he told me what little he knew: that the casualties were "one white man and one white woman." My heart stopped – Kathleen was the only white woman in the delegation.

I went into shock, which manifested itself as autopilot. I was, in my wife's absence, the most senior UN representative in the country. I needed to inform Headquarters. I needed to see the President. I needed to organize a rescue mission. Correction – a rescue and recovery mission.

To this day I wonder at where it came from, this capacity to respond according to protocol despite the traumatic realization that my wife had been killed. Grit? Or shock? I do not recall the details of my encounter with President Buyoya. I only remember the overwhelming emotion when I answered my phone at the end of the meeting to hear Kathleen's beloved voice. She was alive. The white woman who had been killed was the WFP's Saskia von Meijenfeldt, a last-minute addition to the group. Also executed was the UNICEF Representative, Luis Zuniga. All the others had survived, escaping in a moment of confusion created by the security officer to distract the assailants. Kathleen herself had run for three hours through sugar cane fields before she found a factory where she could call me.

I was at the airport that evening to receive my colleagues – the slain and the survivors. I will never forget the sight of Kathleen disembarking. Again in a long flowing dress. This one was covered in the blood of her colleagues. That night, while Kathleen recovered in a hot bath and Daim licked the tears from her cheeks, I took a call from Kofi Annan. The Secretary General conveyed his condolences and asked for a brief report. It was the first of many requests for information and promises to get to the bottom of the attack. In the following weeks, we were to host several delegations come to research the incident. Though there were clear indications that extremists had orchestrated the attack, perhaps even some in Buyoya's circle, there was no indictment of the Burundian President. Instead, we were told to pack up and leave, and the UN moved Burundi into the top security threshold – phase five, evacuation.

But first, there was the closure of mourning our colleagues. The day after the attack, Kathleen and I accompanied the two coffins to Nairobi. We didn't exchange a word through the entire five and a half hour flight. Once we had turned over the bodies to our colleagues in Nairobi, we retreated to a hotel and continued grieving. To this day, Kathleen and I observe the anniversary of that terrible day, October 13, with a mixture of gratitude and grief.

I had experienced many close calls right up till that day. In fact, the prospect of a violent confrontation in my own office, perhaps harming my own staff, is what prevented me from joining the ill-fated delegation to Rutana. In the weeks that followed the ambush, as Kathleen and I fielded the investigations and questions and fact-finders who would ultimately shut down our operation, I found myself reflecting on the times when the larger mission compromised my personal safety. I recalled Artemis Road, the fall of Phnom Penh, Colonel Prachak, the mobs of Mogadishu. I asked myself what my own personal threshold for risk was in commitment to the work of the UN. I asked what the UN's institutional threshold should be for the servants who do its work. I understood that there is little point in trying to reconcile the two; for the tragedies of human loss – civilians who have not been protected, peacekeepers sent to keep a nonexistent peace, or international civil servants whose diplomacy has long lost its immunity in the eyes of aggrieved populations whose deprivation has not yet been addressed by the world community. Tragedy always occurs in the grey zone between security and insecurity, between peace and war, between aid and neglect. Humanity lives in danger zones; humanitarian assistance must too.

I have had the great honor of serving the United Nations for a generation and now I have the pleasure of preparing a new generation to follow. I am the first to concede that the world they live in is no more peaceful than the one I was born into at the twilight of World War. As I write this, violent convulsions in Central Africa, Eastern Europe and the Middle East have forced more than 50 million people from their homes, creating a world refugee crisis unseen since 1945. But aiding the millions around the world affected by conflict, instability and socio-economic inequality is a far more complex and dangerous mission in today's world. The UN, once a proud blue shield, is too often a target; its international civil servants give their lives daily to protect their fellow human beings.

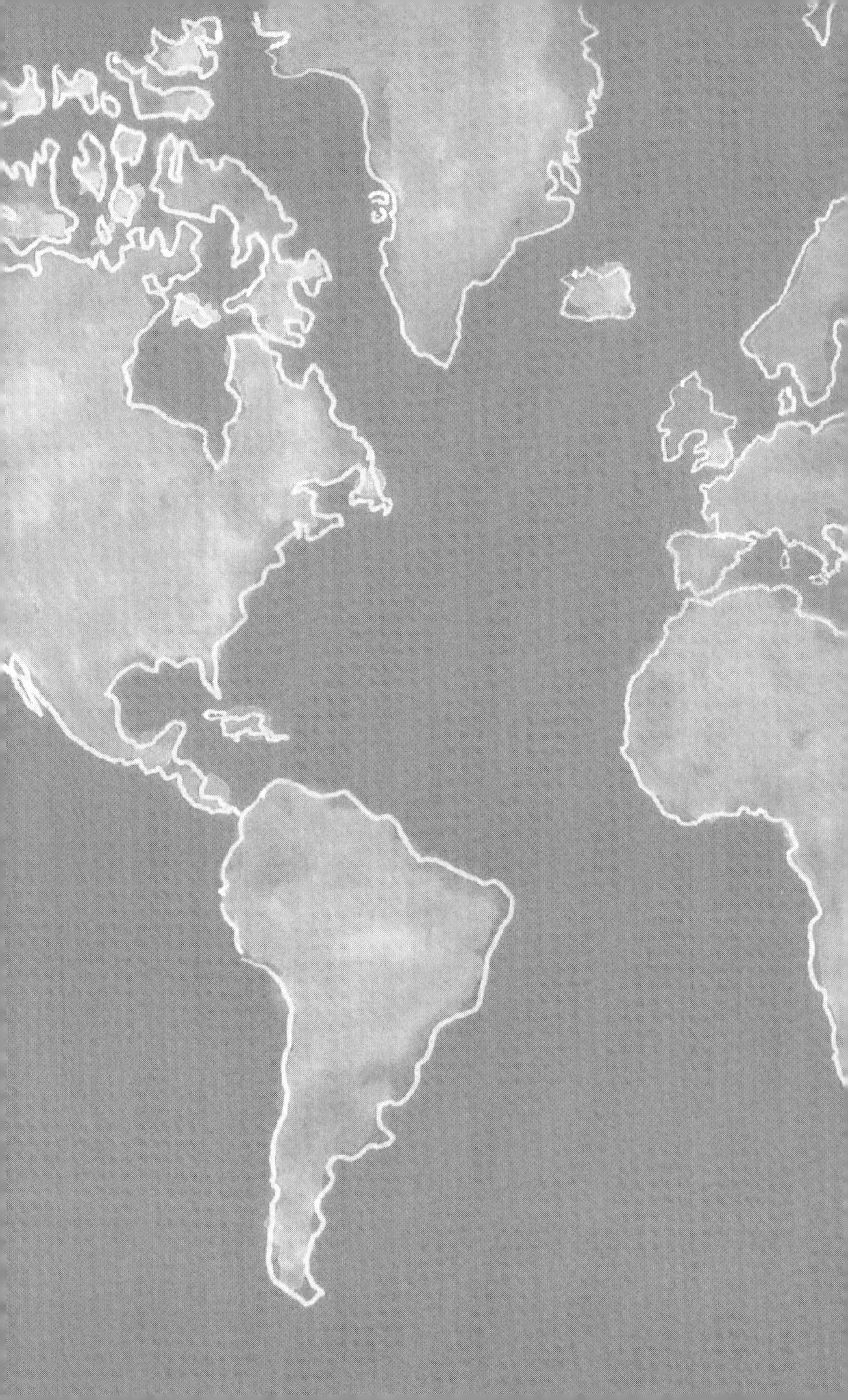

PART 5

PROVIDING FOR PEACEKEEPING

CHAPTER 22

Bhopinder Singh

IN THE COURSE OF MY FOUR DECADES at the United Nations, I have served with dozens of heroes in the field of humanitarian aid. I am grateful to them for reasons beyond the obvious inspiration and education they have provided. Without their shining examples, I would be less equipped to provide my students and other aspiring humanitarian workers with models of excellence: living breathing change-makers who have challenged disease, disaster and conflict and come out winners.

Among those mentors and colleagues to whom I owe thanks, there is one man in particular whom I wish to single out as I near the last chapter of my tale: Bhopinder Singh, whose singular organization, a small non-profit group working in India to protect the elderly, has granted me the opportunity to pay back the debt I owe the world for allowing me to learn so much on its dime. For it is only now that I have shed my official badge as a United Nations servant that I see clearly that I am greatly indebted to the organization. Sure, I gave it the best years of my life, but the hard work that I was entrusted to do as a UN worker has given me more personal satisfaction than I can ever repay.

I am not a religious man, but when I look back at my life, I feel blessed. I feel that I was anointed to see the world, touch a few lives, and bail a few buckets from the endless sea of need that humankind recycles in its own way. To some extent, humanitarian work is akin to missionary work. They both demand a faith deeper than a paycheck. I am enriched by having my faith in the UN and its ideals tested over and over and still emerging strong. And I feel compelled to give thanks for that affirmation in a way that a non-spiritual but deeply moved man can; some call it karma; I call it payback.

As I write this, I am exercising payback through the wonderful organization headed by Bhopinder and Winnie Singh, called Maitri India. This is an organization devoted to caring for elderly women who have been cast out by their families, providing a loving home and social services for a vulnerable and sadly neglected population. And it does more: It promotes public health, educational access, and legal advocacy across India, championing human rights and human dignity. These are missions that are near to my heart, and I am honored to serve Maitri's geographically limited, but broad-focus work. It is an opportunity that arose from a different objective – one with broad geographic parameters but a very targeted focus: enlisting UN peacekeepers in the fight against HIV.

I first met Bhopinder in 2004. Singh was a lieutenant general of the Indian Army, one of the largest in the world. At the time I met him, he commanded the Assam Rifles, India's highly respected security force. In the years since we met, we have discovered any number of shared interests and mutual experiences, from military disciplines to peacekeeping to fine food. But the topic that most consumed India and the United Nations at the time of our meeting was the scourge of AIDS.

CHAPTER 23

An International Security Risk

BY 1999, THE HIV VIRUSs had infected more than 20 million people worldwide; but the response to AIDS, the wasting disease that had killed more than four million was a mix of panic, defeatism and underfunded efforts. The virus bedeviled health workers with its lack of a cure and its insistent spread (who can stop sex?), and the disease burdened its victims further with social stigma.

Researchers were in agreement on the potential horrors of HIV/AIDS, but even the direst predictions failed to forecast just how devastating the short-term impact might be – particularly in Sub-Saharan Africa, where HIV/AIDS is now the leading cause of death

For the first decade of the epidemic, the UN was as halting in its response as any other government or medical group. The World Health Organization was the natural home for AIDS work at the UN, but it initially limited its action to a few international conferences, even excusing itself from further activity in an internal memo in 1983 with the assurance that the disease "is being well taken care of by some of the richest countries in the world where there is the manpower and the know-how and where most of the patients are to be found."

Such a dismissive response was, of course, impossible to support once the medical science community understood that a far greater caseload was affected by the virus: the focus shifted from western homosexuals to the entire adolescent and adult population of Sub-Saharan Africa. Like the problems wrought by climate change, HIV/AIDS today is a scourge that affects smaller, underdeveloped countries disproportionately, but requires the resources and political will of the industrialized world to combat it. The UN resolved to dedicate additional resources and personnel, but more importantly, to broaden the stakeholders of its AIDS directive to include non-state actors into its structure. Thus was born UNAIDS, a consortium governed by UN agencies including UNICEF, UNDP and WHO and growing to encompass more, plus governmental and non-governmental entities. Established in 1996, UNAIDS identified six objectives: to provide global leadership in response to the epidemic; to promote global consensus on policy; to help implement policies at the country level; to strengthen national capacities to implement policy; to promote broad-based political and social mobilization; and to advocate greater global commitment at global and country levels. These objectives read like a common-sense mission statement, but I assure you that blood, sweat and tears were shed to arrive at these objectives. Consensus is the toughest achievement at the United Nations. Consensus on a seemingly impossible task like preventing a mysterious and unflagging killer, the world's youngest and most virulent virus, even more so.

KATHLEEN AND I BOTH JOINED UNAIDS IN 2000. I, for one, was happy to leave warzones, ambushes and death threats behind for the time being and focus on a problem that we might make a lasting contribution to without putting our lives on the line. Our experience in Burundi had shaken me deeply, forcing a new look at our careers, our priorities, and our commitment to our work and to each other. Neither of us could be said to be overly cavalier about the danger we put ourselves in on a regular basis in some of the hottest spots in the world, but in the new millennium, we felt comfortable retiring from hardship posts behind us. There are plenty of challenges in the world to confront without putting one's very life in the ring as well.

We arrived at UNAIDS headquarters in Geneva at an exciting time. After a decade viewed as an inportant but narrowly-conceived public health issue, HIV/AIDS was finally emerging on the agenda of the Security Council'. For the first time, an issue ostensibly related to health and social policy was being treated as a matter of international security. When the Security Council held a special session to discuss HIV/AIDS, culminating in Resolution 1308, it was both a historic moment and a tipping point for the global public health movement.

It would not have happened when it did without Richard Holbrooke, the US Ambassador to the UN, a foreign-policy titan and formidable negotiator. As Jack Chow, one of his colleagues at the State Department, once noted, Holbrooke was of a generation of diplomats "trained in the negotiable currency of the geopolitical realm: missiles, trade agreements, and confidence-building measures -- not condoms or intravenous drug use." To be sure, Holbrooke had made his name negotiating cease-fires and treaties, not making the case for sex-ed. But when Ambassador Holbrooke returned from a twelve-nation tour of Africa in late 1999 insisting that an incurable virus was poised to take more lives than any manmade conflict, he single-handedly altered the dimensions of the fight against AIDS. With President Clinton and Vice-President Gore firmly behind him, Holbrooke wrangled his peers – the most powerful members of the Security Council – into acknowledging the virus as a global threat. The United States cannot always be said to have led the world well or even at all, but at a very crucial moment it led the charge against AIDS.

Holbrooke understood that the United Nations – and more tangibly, the Department of UN Peacekeeping (DPKO)-represented ground zero for the virus. For it was within the capacity of the blue helmets to act as an educated buffer or a human conduit. The HIV virus spreads rapidly and catastrophically anywhere that sex is unprotected and retrovirals unaffordable. But it is particularly corrosive in warzones and areas of political conflict. In such arenas sexual activity spikes for negative reasons, whether due to rape and sexual violence or economic survival. Hence women living in war-torn countries experience higher rates of HIV infection, as do the soldiers they live among. Studies show that the rate of sexually transmitted disease among the military is double or even quintuple that of the general population. And that's in peacetime. The rates during conflict are even higher.

Holbrooke saw this scenario for himself when, not long after spearheading the resolution that would become my professional calling card for the next several years, he travelled to Cambodia. Thirty years after the killing fields and the fall of the Khmer Rouge, UN peacekeepers were finally in force in the country. Along with the 20,000 troops came a parallel influx of sex tourism. Cambodia was experiencing an unprecedented spike in HIV and Holbrooke saw that the UN soldiers were exposed to a new danger: They were in the line of fire of a killer epidemic. What's worse, they could easily become unwitting weapons themselves.

Holbrooke was absolutely right in recognizing the UN peacekeepers - soldiers hired from national armies, some of which are engaged in non-peacekeeping operations elsewhere – as a crucial instrument for prevention. "Otherwise UN peacekeepers will end up causing more deaths than lives they save," he said bluntly. This was the argument that emerged between the painstaking lines of Security Council Resolution 1308, which called for HIV/AIDS testing and training for UN peacekeepers. This was the task that filled the next five years of my life, among the most rewarding of my UN endeavors.

CHAPTER 24

Resolution 1308

THE UNAIDS TEAM THAT KATHLEEN AND I JOINED in Geneva was perhaps the most dynamic and dedicated group of people I have ever worked with. Young, ambitious and hard working, they represented an extraordinary cross-section of people affected by the virus, from survivors to activists and from researchers to diplomats. But among this multi-talented group, few were eager to take on the assignment of addressing HIV/AIDS in the military. The reluctance stemmed in part from unfamiliarity with the demographic. My colleagues could talk a blue streak with health ministers, mothers and village elders about prophylactics and prevention, but they balked at wagging fingers at four-star generals. Even more daunting was the poverty of our mandate. There was absolutely no funding behind the directive to get the world's armies HIV-savvy. The successful administrator of a global training programme for UN peacekeepers would have to wrest both time and money from defense ministers who were already providing DPKO with manpower or peacekeeping budgets.

I looked at these challenges and felt a budding excitement. Ever since my own stint as a peacekeeper in Cyprus, I had retained a real affection and admiration for DPKO – by which I mean for the 100,000 professional soldiers it counts among its ranks.

The makeup of the peacekeeping force had changed radically since my service. In the 21st century, UN troops are deployed almost entirely from the world's poorer countries, their costs subsidized by the industrialized western governments. This is a simple result of global economics. These are the forces that are the most affordable and most willing to take on hardship posts to earn more than they would at home. The rich western countries, on the other hand, contribute the bulk of DPKO's record $8 billion yearly budget but a negligible percentage of troops.

Today's peacekeepers are sent to places far more hostile than Artemis Road. They are tasked with peacebuilding as well as peacekeeping, wearing blue berets as often as blue helmets. They serve six-month deployments far from home, earning wages higher than their own governments can pay, but still minimal when considered in the context of terrorist groups, criminal gangs and ethnic militias that now regularly target UN personnel, armed and not. There have been more than 1,100 deaths among peacekeepers since 2004, the last time the UN authorized a payraise for its seconded troops.

The flaws of the 65-year-old tradition of recruiting peacekeepers from standing armies have become more visible in this less-forgiving environment: the equity of rich countries paying for global security with the blood of less wealthy countries; the role of the permanent members of the Security Council in dispatching brigades with no input from the troops themselves; the perpetual balance of protecting civilian lives without compromising UN authorizations and peacekeepers' lives.

But I remained, then and now, convinced that DPKO provides an invaluable service. I also knew that there would be no DPKO without the contributions of Bangladesh, India, Pakistan, and Nigeria in particular – nations that provided (and continue to provide) the lion's share of peacekeeping troops and faced a disproportionate exposure to HIV. Moreover, these were soldiers who were increasingly tasked with protecting civilians and not just enforcing a cease-fire between uniformed armies as was our mandate in post-war Cyprus.

As I saw it, HIV training for UN peacekeepers was, indeed, a security obligation – a measure of protection for the soldiers, their civilian protectorate, and for the communities they called home. I believed implicitly in

Resolution 1308, the Security Council's request that all member states offer HIV/AIDS testing training to troops scheduled for UN deployment. I offered my credential as a veteran humanitarian expert and I was hired for the job by the Executive Director of UNAIDS, Peter Piot. My title was Director of the Office of AIDS and Security and Humanitarian Response. Kathleen, still my professional as well as personal companion, outranked me as the Deputy Executive Director of UNAIDS.

And so began my five-year adventure equipping UN peacekeepers with information that could save their lives. First and foremost, this was basic information on HIV/AIDS and how it spreads. But like the disease itself, prevention measures touched on much more than sexual behavior. We were addressing domestic violence, substance abuse, as well as human rights and legal procedures. This sensitization, as it is called in the advocacy world, was intended for the men and women wearing the blue berets, with the understanding that back in their home communities, they would pass on their wisdom as respected members of the military. In this way, we were reinforcing prevention within the population of the conflict area as well as in far-flung, often underserved, communities worldwide.

I spent the first year in my new job contacting virtually every Defense Minister on the planet: if they served a rich Western government, I was cajoling them to fund this necessary programme. If they served a developing nation - particularly one of the primary Troop Contributing Countries (TCCs) like India, Pakistan, Bangladesh, Ukraine, and Jordan - I was badgering them to make the programme mandatory for their troops.

Many countries were already doing great work. They didn't simply meet me half way, but had much experience to provide as I crafted a universal approach towards incorporating HIV awareness into the peacekeeping agenda. In Thailand, where more than 5.5 percent of the military was infected with HIV, the Prime Minister had publicly lamented that he had more soldiers dying from disease than from bullets. With his blessing, I worked with the ruling generals on a counseling and testing programme that I am certain saved countless lives and was a major factor reducing the infection rate in the army to just 0.5 percent in a matter of years.

But often the message I brought was not immediately recognized. Even among enlightened, progressive authorities, I sometimes needed to readdress the big picture. In 2002, for example, I travelled to Chile and met with Dr. Michele Bachelet. Now serving her second term as President, Bachelet has also headed the UN's agency for women empowerment. But a dozen years ago this much-respected global leader was unconcerned about the spread of HIV in Chile. When I explained to her that she would be sending troops to Haiti in the near future, where there was a dangerous infection rate, she put away her other papers and began to listen. I told her about the programme's impact in Thailand, and she followed with many questions and thoughts. Our scheduled five-minute meeting turned into an hour-long meeting. Bachelet was on board.

Once I had secured the political support of the governments, I moved on to what generally felt like more familiar terrain - discussions with the military brass. I approached the generals of troop contributing countries with special respect. I assured them of my appreciation of their contributing soldiers as representative of neutrality, stability, protection and order. But that, I noted, did not make them any less susceptible to biology. They too, had sexual relations and brought the results home to their communities and families. Every discussion was different. In some cases I had to overcome real resistance. There were generals with whom I engaged in a benign *machismo*. Not unlike Jim Grant's argument that the strongest dictator was the one who saved the most children's lives, I sometimes argued that the most respected soldier was the one who kept his fellow countrymen healthy, as well as safe.

In most cases, I found a common language with the military officers who had the most to gain from opening the discussion to the rank and file. In Thailand, General Souphong needed no prodding from me. Uganda, also, had declared HIV/AIDS a national security issue before the Security Council named it an international one. Brazil's and Peru's top generals were similarly responsive. They were contributing a disproportionate number of soldiers and consequently seeing more infections among their troops than many countries.

Far and away, the most successful partner I ever encountered in all my negotiations with military men high and low was with General Bhopinder Singh. When I met him in 2004, I was surprised to learn that he had made HIV training and prevention awareness mandatory in his brigade. This despite the fact that Indian society is traditionally conservative and highly averse to public discussion of sexually transmitted diseases. This is changing some today, as the country comes to terms with a recent highly publicized spate of horrific sexual abuse. But India remains a very conservative place, resistant to progressive talk and change. Nonetheless, Singh saw the importance of addressing HIV. Though he was very nearly demoted for it, he pushed the prevention agenda.

But there are only so many Bhopinder Singhs in the world. On some occasions I was told in no uncertain terms what I could do with my training materials. One decade ago, the stigma of AIDS was several orders stronger than even today. As a "dirty disease," that couldn't be discussed without speaking of sexual behaviors, sexual orientation, and contraceptive, it was a delicate subject for Catholic countries, radical Muslim states and any other society that was traditionally terse on such taboo subjects. My expertise was in frank, blunt talk, so the delicacy of discussing HIV was a steep learning curve for me. But I never doubted my authority to insist on a respectful reception from every General I met. Everywhere I announced myself as a former military man and an officer of the United Nations with a political brief: Resolution 1308 had empowered me.

It also gave me a new set of wings and the need for a new passport: I was dispatched all over the world to act as a chief diplomat for our programme. When my advisor in Bangkok informed me that Mongolia had expressed interest in signing a partnership with UNAIDS, I first had to find it on the map. Mongolia was just wrestling itself from the post-Soviet Marxist/Leninist political system. The capital, Ulan Bator, was grey, dark and miserably cold from the relentless wind blowing off the high plateaus. On the streets, everyone dressed in the same dark suits. I met with the Minister of Defense, with whom I exchange perhaps five mutually understood words. He signed the agreement and left the room. My entire mission to Mongolia was over in a matter of minutes. But that signature was all it took to ensure that Mongolia's uniformed military and civilian police would embrace our programme.

Before I left Mongolia I was invited out by one of the local UN staff to visit a yurt where some nomads were staying. We drove for half a day out into the desolate expanse and came upon a place that perfectly matched my imaginations of Genghis Kahn's stomping grounds. We were invited by the inhabitants to admire their horses and share their traditional food and drink. I can't say that I was enamored with the fermented horse milk and unrecognizable spongy substance they called cheese, but I was certainly impressed with the quality of their horses. On my way back to the capital we visited a Buddhist temple. Its immense hall, perhaps four hundred years old, was filled to capacity with monks, humming and praying. That experience alone was worth the long flight across Asia. But I was also glad to return to Geneva with another partner for Resolution 1308.

Perhaps my most successful mission, if success is defined by signatures of support, occurred when I sat down with the police commanders of fifteen separate South Pacific islands and brought them into the HIV troop-training fold over the course of a day. I will be ever grateful to the Australian government for facilitating that scoop. Afterwards, at a reception at the local UNAIDS advisor's home, I was offered a murky liquid called kava. Fiji's traditional drink, kava is highly narcotic drink, producing numbness of the tongue and, in excess, your entire body. I had seen the damaging social effects of the drink on the streets in Fiji. The next day I experienced the rather violent after-effects myself.

THE BELLWETHER EVENT FOR AIDS PREVENTION came in July 2001, when the UN held its first-ever Special Session on AIDS: UNGASS was its less-than-melodious acronym. The middle of summer is not necessarily the most auspicious time to hold a high-level meeting of global ramifications in New York City. But the stakes were high.

I was dispatched to New York to oversee security, a three-ring circus that slowed Midtown Manhattan to a crawl and gave me a headache for nearly two weeks. I quickly saw why the local New Yorkers so loathed the UN meetings. Even pre-9/11, the security was tremendous; Streets were cordoned off for blocks and blocks and the traffic was a colossal nightmare. But I was impressed by the humor and professional manner of the New York Police department, and I developed a great rapport with the UN Security detail and the New York City branch of the FBI.

Meanwhile, within the UNAIDS Secretariat, my team and Kathleen's belabored, with a heavy deadline hanging over us, the document that was to be presented to the General Assembly. During long, hot sessions with high stakes, we gathered leaders of all stripes to discuss that most touchy of subjects – sex. It was difficult to find a common language with fundamentalists, orthodox believers, and Islamic states when it came to terms like *sex trafficking, transgender, prostitution* and *homosexuality*. I recall my desperation when I called the Swedish ambassador at midnight to say that we could not even get the word "condom" into the document. Messages were couriered all over the city as people were sent to deliver food, drink, toothbrushes and toothpaste to the seated delegations. In the evening many of the Western delegations assigned junior staff members to attend, while the African and Arab csent their highest ranking ambassadors, knowing that they could have their voices heard at these late night sessions.

In the end, our perseverance paid off. In June 2001, the General Assembly adopted our document as the basis for a Declaration of Commitment, another landmark resolution that would take its place in the history of global public health.

Two years later I was back in New York, chasing my tail because of a minor oversight that reminded me what I loved about being a roving ambassador rather than a gopher of Turtle Bay. This time the hang-up in our working group came when we were informed of a technical dispute between Greece and Macedonia. Our presentation, you see, made a reference to the country of Macedonia, an entity that the Greeks do not recognize. And since the head of the Security Council at that time was the Ambassador of Greece, this constituted a major wrench in the works. My undaunted team worked through the entire night to correcting the offending line in more than a hundred already-printed and bound copies of our document to read "the former Yugoslavian Province of Macedonia."

With the corrected progress report distributed to the members of the Council, we briefed the delegates for the final time on the progress of our programme and we received unanimous support, a rare achievement. When Kofi Annan gave his accolades for this programme, I looked up at my colleagues in the gallery, and all fourteen people gave the thumbs up. I was glowing with pride.

By 2001 I had a small but effective staff of seven people responsible for HIV-training programmes from East Timor to Haiti. With funding support from the governments of Norway, Ireland and Sweden, we were able to create standard issue emergency wallets with prophylactic information (as well as an actual prophylactic) that were included in the uniforms of all UN peacekeepers. We were also able to hire trainers from an array of professions, cultural background and countries including China, Congo, France, United States, Uruguay, Ireland, Serbia, and Uganda.

I attended some of these trainings, where I observed some interesting phenomena: First, that the soldiers of the world had a shockingly rudimentary understanding of basic sexual hygiene. Ninety percent of the troops we were hiring as UN peacekeepers did not know how to properly put on a condom. Our educators used a banana and cucumber as visual aides to demonstrate, which brings me to the second revelation: that some lessons were more lasting when delivered by a woman than a man. I will never forget the attractive nurse who had a room of Uruguayan soldiers (devout Catholics, all) in her thrall as she wielded her banana. Nor the fierce Nigerian doctor who reduced a brigade of blustering soldiers to blubber with her description's of the disease's ferocity. Thirdly, it was interesting to note that the training programme had a greater impact than many civilian programmes, since the trainees were already in the mindset of taking marching orders.

After one year we reported back to the General Assembly: Hundreds of soldiers had received our training and we had advisors on staff in Sierra Leone, Liberia, Congo, Somalia and East Timor. After the second year, we were commended and rewarded with participation and support from the Pentagon where the Assistant Secretary of Defense, Bear McConnell, welcomed our mission and helped form an International Task Force on HIV/AIDS with his military diplomatic connections. The involvement of the Pntagon was a watershed development for me, for my team, and for UNAIDS more broadly. For starters, there was the imposing presence of the massive building, off-limits for most of the world. We held several meetings in its maze, the last of which took place just weeks before a hijacked jet crashed into one of its five flanks on September 11th. I co-chaired the Task Force on AIDS and Security together with Commander

Rick Schaeffer of the US Nacy. When not meeting at the Pentagon, our group met in other pillars of power: at West Point Academy, at the Thai Army Headquarters, or at the UNAIDS Headquarters in Geneva. I was also invited, in that second year of our programme, to participate in one of NATO's "war games" in Heidelberg, Germany.

By our third year, we could report that 100 countries were enrolled in training. I had raised $18 million dollars and signed agreements with twenty Defense Ministers worldwide. More tangibly, we could see the fruits of our efforts in the breast pocket of every UN Peacekeeper under contract -- the plastic wallet with HIV prevention tips and an emergency condom was now standard issue along with the peacekeepers' blue beret and armband.

FOR SOME YEARS AFTER I RETIRED from the United Nations in 2006, I continued to work with UNAIDS as a consultant because I found the work rewarding and because I saw more progress to be made. Today, I contribute within a smaller environment, through Maitri India, which is doing wonderful work with vulnerable communities in a nation that is on the forefront of affordable treatment. But I must say that I have never have I felt quite so engaged in the battle as when I was advancing the education agenda among the soldiers whose job was to provide a bulwark against all sorts of encroaching danger.

I am reminded of the significance of that work every time I read about the sacrifices made by emergency responders in Liberia, Guinea and Sierra Leone. The peril that these brave heroes face daily to attend to, and tragically, to dispose of, the victims of Ebola is truly sobering. I salute these men and women with a brimming heart. They need support, these first responders. Not least, the knowledge, protective clothing and the talking points to share with frightened communities about the truths of transmission and prevention. I have seen the difference such training can make.

By increasing the awareness level at UN bases around the world, I truly felt I had boots on the ground in the battle against AIDS. And that has always been where my feet are most comfortable ... on the ground, in the field, where they might leave lasting, if muddy, tracks.

EPILOGUE

NOT LONG AGO, I ATTENDED THE FIFTIETH ANNIVERSARY of my graduating class of the Royal Marines. Over a late summer weekend in August, about a dozen of us old-timers relived forgotten jokes, unforgettable trials and wondered, "what became of so and so?"

Many of my old cohort, men who have distinguished themselves in careers just as global and unpredictable as my own, wanted to know my thoughts on the endless bad news that make up our headlines today: unrest in the Middle East; proxy war in Ukraine; near genocidal conditions in Southern Sudan and Central African Republic; a lost generation in Syria; the rise of ISIS and its ilk; and the onslaught of Ebola.

I was honest. I told them that I have never seen the world so troubled. I recognize many of these troubles: They are the same problems I confronted with my colleagues at UNICEF and at UNHCR.

Whether the issue is the Security Council's tying itself up in knots over the complex need to halt ISIS while not propping up Syria's Assad, or the criticism laid at the WHO for its belated response to Ebola, I can commiserate. In Cambodia we struggled to provide for thousands of victims of a regime that we were legitimizing as we did so. On the border, we were forever caught off guard by things unanticipated, from disease to insurgency.

As I observe the continued deterioration of society in Chad and Burundi, I remember the efforts of my teams to promote progress in fractured communities led by shortsighted, corrupt governments. The brutality and bloodshed in South Sudan and Central African Republic are particularly saddening for me, having once seen light at the end of these tunnels.

Even as our collective efforts (and they are significant in the 21st century, encompassing far more financial and human resources than fifty years ago) to advance health, education and rights pay off, famine persists, conflict persists, refugees persist. Fifty million people, their present precarious and their future bleak, are displaced and on the move today.

And then there is the question of the impact of the UN two generations after its founding. It has weathered scandals, absorbed defeats and seen its shield turned into a target. When I read about fourteen peacekeepers slain in Mali, I think of Artemis Road. What if I, a young platoon commander had failed those men? If they had died, would their lives have been in vain? Every day, aid workers are captured, tortured and killed in the line of duty - some in their communities, others far from home. Whether they are grassroots community health workers, idealistic new recruits of international NGOs, or veteran UN workers, I always bow my head in honor of my slain colleagues in Burundi, Luis and Saskia, and in tribute to the sacrifice of all the other men and women who have lost their lives in the line of duty.

Faced with the human, environmental and economic crises of the early 21st century, it is all too easy to despair. So I rely on the hindsight of history to remind me of the importance of the UN – no, the absolute potential of the UN – in preventing the worst. Without the diplomatic channels of United Nations, it is very likely that the Cuban Missile Crisis would not have been resolved peaceably. Without the lifesaving agencies of the United Nations, hundreds of thousands of people would have died in northern Thailand in 1979, in Ethiopia in 1983, and in South Sudan today. That the UN can still throw its lifeline, even after it has been rejected or proven too short like in Rwanda or in Darfur, is significant.

Finally, the development power of the United Nations cannot be discounted. It is the work and the workers of the UN that have raised life expectancies, reduced child and maternal mortality, championed human rights, and strengthened governments' commitment and capacity to serve its people from Brazil to Burundi to Borneo.

I do worry. The world is changing too rapidly for a lumbering bureaucracy to keep up. The UN as a system, needs a massive update for the 21st century. It needs to reflect, in human terms, the new geopolitical reality, in which the original five victors of World War II no longer have a monopoly on geopolitical and economic power. In this era, the biggest existential threat to humanity is not a belligerent army (even one with the bloody-minded fanaticism of Islamic State); it is climate change and the potential impacts of natural disaster, epidemics and resource scarcity brought on by climate change. If the UN is to present a credible fight against these threats, it must give more decision making power to the members most threatened. The allies who defeated Hitler and were thereby granted irrefutable preeminence on the Security Council should be reconsidered, for they have long since ceded their shared interest in the global good. It is time to empower new leaders at the helm.

And there are many other ways that the UN must reform to become nimbler, more innovative, less entwined in red tape and protocol.

The question is: *Can it do it?*

My answer after four decades of observation of the good, the bad, and the ugly, is *yes*. I say "yes" because I have seen dedicated international servants who believe in the fundamental good of the United Nations' mission working together with young leaders and respected elders to benefit humanity. I have seen this cooperation and determination at work even in the most trying of environments. And as long as that idealism and fellowship exists, even in small amounts, the world will provide ample grit to make it take root and grow.

ACKNOWLEDGMENTS

This book was not an impromptu decision. I have pondered the idea of recording the highlights of my United Nations career for many years. I credit the enthusiastic interest of those students who took my class on global health and security at the George Washington University as the catalyst I needed to commit to the task.

My niece Claire Cravero was the first to help me unpack four decades of stories and place them on a timeline. Claire, a Peace Corps volunteer like me, shares the hope, optimism and spirit that I felt when I first entered the world of international development. It was a pleasure to have such an avid scribe and cheerleader as I put pen to paper.

Pen to paper was a start, but without the editorial skills of Elizabeth Kiem I would not have gotten the paper to press. Elizabeth, another former UNICEF employee, brought to the task of shaping my stories a familiarity with the mission and language of the United Nations while retaining my own voice. I am grateful and privileged to have had an advisor of her caliber, creativity, experience … and patience.

Thanks to Adam Fifield and Maggie Black for reading early drafts and providing valuable input. Adam's insight into the personalities of Jim Grant's UNICEF and Maggie's detailed knowledge of UN history and mechanics were particularly valuable.

Thanks also to Gia Giasullo, who designed the book cover to cover; to Caroline Jacobssen for help in preparing the photographs; and to Lynda Gray for her eagle eye as a copy-editor.

In addition to those who helped write and publish this book, I wish to acknowledge those who made my life one worth writing about. In particular: Sir Robert Jackson, Martti Ahtisaari, Jim Grant, Charles Egger, Bernard Kouchner and Richard Holbrooke. These men helped shape my career and put me on the right path when I strayed at a fork in the road. I consider them heroes, mentors and friends.

To acknowledge every colleague with whom I have had the pleasure of working would require more pages than there are in this book. Along the way, I have met countless men and women who have worked tirelessly to make the world a fairer, safer place. Many have given their lives to this goal. Most will never have the privilege of writing down their experiences. Let this book be a tribute to them all.

In particular I wish to acknowledge: Pamela Reitemeir, Tanny Noorlander, Rose Awad Toma, Roberto Bertucci, Hedda Mattson and Jocelyn Pierre, Peter Weineger, Esin Güllü, Rade Mihailovich, Luciello Ramirez, Sami Behran, Jim Sherry and Colonel Kitty.

My deepest thanks to the women who moved mountains in the Office for HIV/AIDS and Security: Gael Lescornec, Sinead Ryan-Andersen, Andrea Boccardi, Eni Nene, Nertila Tavenxi, Jelena Vledicic, Roxanne Bazergan.

And of course, my unending gratitude to Kathleen, the most outstanding woman I have ever met and the leading light in my personal and professional life for the last twenty years.

Ulf T. Kirstoffersson
January 2015

INDEX

Abramowitz, Morton, 53, 55
Acar, Joseph, 22, 27-28
AIDS (see HIV/AIDS)
Al-Bashir, Omar Hassan, 36
Amin, Mohammed, 13
Angka, 28
Annan, Kofi, 49-50, 75, 163-164, 175, 193
Aranyaprathet, 9-10, 28, 39-52
Arkhipov, Vasily, 69, 71
Artemis Road, 80-83
Behran, Sami, 51
Bernadotte, Folke, 75
Bertolaso, Guido, 49, 126
Bjork, Wendy, 22, 27
Blue helmets, berets (see DPKO and United Nations Peacekeepers)
Cambodia
    killing fields, 10-11, 28-29, 34, 37-39, 58, 186
    "Land Bridge" 53-58, 102-104, 122
        military, 18, 21-25
        Prince Sihanouk, 21, 40
        refugee crisis, 9-10, 21-30, 39-52
        role in Vietnam War 13-15, 21
        UNICEF in 21-30, 41-48, 53-58
Carter, Jimmy, 121
Carter, Rosalyn, 48
Chad, 106-107, 122-126, 190-130, 198
Clinton, Bill, 163, 185
Cold War, 2, 14, 37, 68-73, 83, 87-88, 147-148, 174-177, 184, 187-189
Cravero, Kathleen, 146, 165, 170-171
Cuban Missile Crisis, 68-71
Cyprus, 79-86, 188
Dallaire, Romeo, 161-163
De Mello, Sergio, 50
DPKO (Department of Peacekeeping Operations)
    and AIDS, 182-195
    casualties, 19, 82, 84-85, 176, 188, 198
        in Cyprus, 79-86
        in Darfur, 149, 198
        in Rwanda, 161-164
        in Somalia, 155
        in South Sudan, 85, 164
        in Syria, 71, 83, 164
        training, 74
Egger, Charles, 32, 43
Ethiopia
    famine, 48, 113-120, 198
    UNICEF in, 114-120
    revolution of, 114
Geldof, Bob, 113
Genocide
    in Burundi, 50, 139, 171
    in Cambodia, 56, 139
    in Rwanda, 139, 161-164
Grant, Jim, 32-36, 106, 115-125, 129-130, 139, 140-142
Greenstock, Jeremy, 2
Habré, Hissene, 106, 128-130
Hammarskjöld, Dag, 65, 70, 75-77, 87
HIV/AIDS, 167, 182-195
Humanitarian aid, 1-3, 10-11, 14-15, 22, 29-35, 39-43, 45, 53-58, 111-120, 131-139, 147-152, 166-167, 173-174, 178, 181-182
Ignatieff, Paul, 19-22, 27-28, 42
International Committee of the Red Cross (ICRC), 10, 42, 54, 101, 23-24, 39, 156-157
Jackson, Robert, 51-52
Kagame, Paul, 168
Kennedy, John F., 69, 87
Khmer Rouge
    brutality, 9-11, 28
    killing fields, 25-29, 34, 37-39
    UNICEF and, 21-30, 41-48, 53-58
Koh, Tommy, 56-57
Ki-Moon, Ban, 75-76, 85
Kilimanjaro, 17, 94-95
Kitty, Colonel, 46-47
Labouisse, Henry, 14, 34, 38, 41-43
Laos, 31-35
Malloch-Brown, Mark, 49-50
Malmö, 65-66
Mengistu Haile Mariam, Colonel, 114-120
Mogadishu, 155-159

NGO, non-governmental organizations
    in Ethiopia, 115, 119
    in Phnom Penh, 24, 26
    on Thai/Cambodia border, 43, 48
Palme, Olaf, 87
Pathet Lao, 31-33
Peace Corps, 87-97
Peacekeeping (see DPKO)
Phnom Penh
    evacuation from, 23, 26-28
    UNICEF in, 21-30, 53-58
Prachak Sawaengchit, Col., 46-47
Refugee camps
    in Ethiopia, 116
    in Kenya, 152-152
    in Uganda, 164-169
    on Thai/Cambodia border, 41-58
    urban refugees in Burundi, 174-175
R2P or Responsibility to Protect, 164
Rwanda, 71, 82, 161-164, 168, 171-172
Scheller, Ferdinand, 26, 28
Sahel, 121-130
Seng Path, 34, 111
Somalia, 137, 145-159, 194
Soviet Union, 14, 31, 68-71
Shawcross, William, 38, 44
Stevenson, Adlai, 70-71
Sudan, 131-139
Suez Crisis, 76-77
Sweden, 65-66, 70, 73-75, 87-91, 104, 166
Tanzania
    Swedish peace corps in, 87-89
    Selous Game Reserve, 88-90
    ujamaa socialist experiment, 88-93
Thailand
    role in Vietnam War, 9, 37
    role in Cambodian border crisis, 37, 40, 45-48
UNAIDS, 125, 184, 187, 189-195
UNICEF
    executive directors, 14, 34-35, 41-43, 106, 115-125, 129-130, 132-136, 139, 142
    formation of, 13-14
    in Cambodia, 21-30, 41-48, 53-58, 100-101
    in Chad, 106-107, 122-130
    in Ethiopia, 114-120
    in Laos, 31-35
    in Sudan, 131-139
    in Vietnam, 33
    Office of Emergency Operations, 131, 145
United Nations
    Charter, 1, 70, 156, 162
    General Assembly, 3, 41, 56-57, 139, 144, 164, 192-194
    peacekeeping operations (see DPKO)
    Secretaries General, 42, 49-50, 52, 75-76, 105, 163-164, 175, 193
    Security Council, 50, 56-57, 69-71, 76, 83, 138, 155-157, 161-164, 185-186, 188-190, 197
United Nations High Commissioner of Refugees (UNHCR)
    in Burundi, 171-177
    in Kenya, 149-153
    in Somalia, 148, 156-159
    in Thailand, 41-43, 45, 49
    in Uganda, 165-169
    joining, 144-146
USAID, 21, 31
Vaccination, 107, 122-130, 132, 138, 149
Van Seran, 40, 44, 105
Waldheim, Kurt, 42, 52, 75, 105
Wallenberg, Raoul, 68, 75
World Food Programme, 42

Ulf T. Kristoffersson is an international civil servant with more than four decades experience in the United Nations. He has held high-level positions with DPKO, UNICEF, UNHCR and UN-AIDS and responded to humanitarian emergencies from Southeast Asia to Central Africa. He is currently a visiting professor at the University of Lund in Sweden and the Chair of the Maitri Foundation in India.

Mr. Kristoffersson lives in Geneva and Sweden with his wife Kathleen Cravero-Kristoffersson. His has two daughters and three grandchildren, all living in Stockholm.